DATE DUE

Reconstruction

America After the Civil War

Black men, most of whom had spent their entire lives as slaves, won the
right to vote during Reconstruction.

Reconstruction

America After the Civil War

Zak Mettger

LODESTAR BOOKS
Dutton   New York

to Sue and Phil Mettger, who did a
better job than they think

Library of Congress Cataloging-in-Publication Data

Mettger, Zak.
    Reconstruction—America after the Civil War / Zak Mettger. — 1st ed.
      p.   cm. — (Young readers' history of the Civil War)
    Includes bibliographical references and index.
    ISBN 0-525-67490-X
    1. Reconstruction—Juvenile literature.   2. United States—Politics and government—1865–1877—Juvenile literature.   [1. Reconstruction.   2. United States—History—1865–1898.]   I. Title.   II. Series.
E668.M56   1994
973.8'1—dc20   93-44665
                                                                                  CIP
                                                                                  AC

Published in the United States by Lodestar Books,
an affiliate of Dutton Children's Books,
a division of Penguin Books USA Inc.
375 Hudson Street
New York, N.Y. 10014

Published simultaneously in Canada by
McClelland & Stewart, Toronto

Series development/book production: Laing Communications Inc.,
    Redmond, Washington.
Editorial management: Christine Laing
Research/writing assistance: Rebecca Gleason
Design: Sandra Harner

Printed in the U.S.A.   First Edition   10 9 8 7 6 5 4 3 2 1

✦ Contents ✦

Cities throughout America's South were reduced to rubble during the Civil War. This ghostly scene is in Richmond, Virginia, after its surrender to the North.

ONE

• *An Uncertain Future* •

For four years, the guns and cannon had pounded the cities, homes, bridges, and railways of the South. But now, in the spring of 1865, the weapons of the Union and Confederate armies were silent. The Civil War, one of the bloodiest conflicts in American history, was over.

The war had started in 1861 when eleven southern states, worried about threats to a way of life based on slavery, broke away from the United States and formed a separate country—the Confederate States of America. The North went to war to preserve the Union and stop the spread of slavery.

At first, both sides expected a short battle and decisive victory. But the fighting that pitted Northerners against Southerners raged on month after month, year after year, from Gettysburg, Pennsylvania, into the heartland of the South. By the time the war had ended with a Union victory, more than 620,000 Americans lay dead. Thousands

Note to Readers: As you read this book, you will come across quotes that contain misspelled words and ungrammatical language. This is because many people of the time did not have much education, and did the best they could to invent spellings. Also, journalists of the era tried to record the way people spoke, and spelled words to show how the speaker pronounced them. In cases where the words were very hard to understand, we have corrected the spelling.

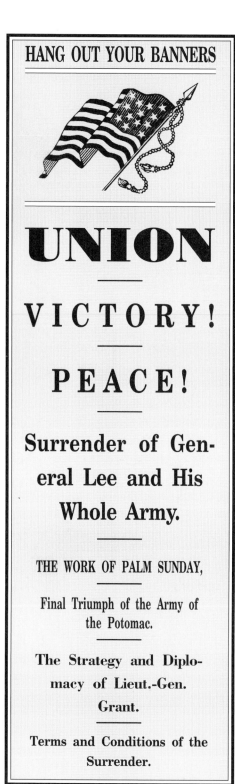

HANG OUT YOUR BANNERS

UNION

VICTORY!

PEACE!

Surrender of General Lee and His Whole Army.

THE WORK OF PALM SUNDAY,

Final Triumph of the Army of the Potomac.

The Strategy and Diplomacy of Lieut.-Gen. Grant.

Terms and Conditions of the Surrender.

of the surviving soldiers were crippled by wounds, disease, or the hardships suffered in prisoner-of-war camps.

Families, black and white, free and slave, were torn apart. Nearly everyone had lost a husband, son, father, or brother to the war.

In the South, where most of the war was fought, entire cities were reduced to piles of ash and shattered brick, and countless men, women, and children were without food or shelter. The farms and plantations that had fed the region's people, and produced the cotton, sugar, and other goods prized by the North and Europe, were blackened and bare.

But on those plantations, the four million black men, women, and children who had lived in slavery greeted the end of the war—and the beginning of freedom—with great joy. For the first time, they could dream of things other Americans had taken for granted: to have a home, a vegetable garden, and a field for crops; to send their children to school instead of to the cotton fields; to read and write their own names. After the powerlessness of slavery, they yearned for the right to vote, to run for political office, to have a say in their country's government.

Many white Southerners, however, found it difficult to accept that their slaves were free. Slavery had been an

The four years of bloodshed drew to a close with the surrender of Confederate General Robert E. Lee and his army on April 9, 1865.

Among the hundreds of thousands who died during the Civil War were these Confederate soldiers, killed in battle at Spotsylvania, Pennsylvania.

unquestioned part of southern society, and the foundation of the region's plantation system. Now, suddenly, the black men and women whom planters had considered their personal property were making their own decisions. They were refusing to work in the fields, leaving plantations, and planning their own futures. Plantation owners were dumbfounded—did the freed slaves have no loyalty or affection for the masters who had fed them, clothed them, cared for them when they were sick? And, even worse, did freedmen and women think they were now equal to white Southerners?

In the North, there was turmoil as well. Many Northerners wanted to punish the southern rebels by taking away their lands, and, in some cases, their lives. Other Northerners wanted to put the harsh feelings of the war behind them, reunite the nation, and help the South get back on its feet again.

Throughout the United States, and especially in the South, people looked to the future with mingled feelings of fear, hope, and uncertainty. This troubling post-Civil War period, which lasted from

1865 to 1877, became known as Reconstruction. It held great promise, great surprises, and great grief for many Americans.

◆   ◆   ◆

In Columbia, South Carolina, eighteen-year-old Emma LeConte had never been so unhappy. The Civil War was over—and the North had won. The young white woman could not bear the thought of Confederate defeat. "*We* give up to the Yankees!" she wrote in her diary on April 16. "How *can* it be?"

Emma's adored cousins, Johnny and Julian, had returned from the battlefield, but her joy at seeing them again was mixed with sorrow. "For four years we have looked forward to . . . the day

Emma LeConte and her family may have walked past these very ruins in Columbia, South Carolina.

when the troops would march home," she wrote in her diary. "We would have waited many years if only we could have received them back triumphant."

On a moonlit walk with her family through the streets of Columbia, which had been battered by the armies of Union General William Tecumseh Sherman, Emma was struck by the cruel contrast between the lovely May evening and the ruins of the once-beautiful capital city. "As far as the eye could reach," she recorded in her diary, all she and her family could see were "spectre-like chimneys and the shattered walls."

The LeContes had little time to contemplate the destruction; they had more practical worries. Emma's father, Joseph, had been a respected teacher, scientist, and part-owner of a large plantation in Liberty County, Georgia. He lost his teaching job at South Carolina College when Union soldiers closed the school. And the plantation no longer provided the family with any income: There was no money to buy seeds for crops, and there were no slaves to plant or tend the fields.

Like Joseph LeConte, many plantation owners struggled to find the money to feed their families, repair their damaged homes, replace their livestock, plant new crops, and pay their debts. Planters who managed to restock their plantations still had to find enough laborers to sow and harvest their crops. Eager to taste freedom, black field hands were abandoning plantations. Black house servants, too, were departing, leaving no one to look after the planters' children or to do the cooking, cleaning, washing, and sewing.

Faced with having to do this work themselves, the plantation owners and their families at first felt helpless. Most had never tilled a field, scrubbed a pot, or sewn a stitch. "I never did a day's work in my life, and don't know how to begin," a South Carolina planter told a northern journalist. Another woman moaned to a reporter, "Ladies of the North, if they lose their servants, can do their own work; but we can't, we can't."

For Emma LeConte, who had been raised in luxury, life seemed hard during the early years after the Civil War. But at least she and her family had a roof over their heads, food to eat, and clothes to wear. Thousands of other southern families, white and black, did not even have that. Countless people starved to death or died of exposure and disease in the first two years after the war. Without rations distributed by federal military officials, northern missionaries, and aid societies, even more would have perished.

Conditions among the South's non-slaveholding farmers, most of whom lived outside the plantation belt, were especially dire. These farmers usually owned small parcels of land that, even in the best of years, produced only enough to feed their families, with perhaps a little left over to sell or trade. Because every family member was needed to work on the farm, the loss of a husband or brother in the war plunged many small farmers into debt and poverty. In Georgia, for example, stories of "extreme want and destitution" among white farming families and of "hundreds of widows and orphans on the verge of starvation" reached relief agents.

Beyond concerns about day-to-day survival—where to find work, food, and housing—many white Southerners worried about the future. The old laws and rules of the South had been swept away. Who would make the new ones? Would Southerners be treated as a conquered people—forced to rejoin the Union and live according to "Yankee" rules? Would Northerners—or perhaps even freedmen—be put in charge of their state governments?

Already, rumors were circulating that black Union soldiers would be stationed in southern cities to keep the peace. "Have we not suffered enough?" wrote Emma LeConte in her diary after learning that black troops were on their way to Columbia. For Emma, who

Unable to make a living on their land anymore, these non-slaveholding farmers have become refugees.

had heard wild stories that black soldiers stationed in Charleston were perpetrating "every barbarity" on the white citizens, "the very thought is enough to make one shudder."

Most white Southerners shared Emma's fear. It was hard for them to imagine what life would be like now that black men and women were free. Would the former slaves be permitted to vote? To own land? Most important, would they continue to work on the plantations, where their labor was desperately needed? Fewer whites spoke openly of an even deeper fear: that newly freed slaves might turn on their former owners and violently avenge the years of humiliation and mistreatment.

Overwhelmed by uncertainty, many white Southerners sustained themselves by clinging to their "deep and abiding" hatred of the North, "the despoiler of the South, the destroyer of sacred institutions and [a] treasured way of life," as one woman put it. A Columbia hotelkeeper told a northern reporter that in one night the Yankees had reduced him to poverty. But, he said, "they've left me one inestimable privilege—to hate 'em. I git up at half-past four in the morning and sit up till twelve at night, to hate 'em."

Other Southerners, such as Kate Cumming, believed that former

In this idealized painting, *The Lost Cause*, a Confederate soldier mourns family members who have died during his long absence. In the South especially, many soldiers returned from years of fighting to find their homes in shambles, their fields overgrown, and their loved ones starving, dead, or simply gone.

These black and white Southerners are united by the hunger and despair that overran the defeated South.

Confederates should concentrate on healing and rebuilding. A staunch supporter of the Confederacy, Cumming had worked as a nurse throughout the war and had seen the grim results of the conflict in the face of every soldier she treated.

Cumming did not ask Southerners to forget all they had suffered, but "to stop useless recriminations. . . . A truly great man does not know revenge," she said. "His soul rises above it as something fit for meaner minds. So with nations. Leave our statesmen to settle our difficulties."

Once they recovered from the shock of the Confederacy's defeat, most southern planters did attempt to put the war behind them and get on with the business of living. Georgia planter Howell Cobb acknowledged in September 1865 that the "present is a blank and the future as full of doubts and perplexities as our worst enemy could desire it to be." Nevertheless, he advised his fellow planters "to yield to our destiny with the best possible grace. . . . and make up their minds to live out their future days in the Old Union."

Rebel soldiers also felt the South's defeat keenly. But most were glad when the war ended. They had seen more than enough of fighting and death, and wanted most of all to return home to their "dear ones."

Union soldiers, too, welcomed the end of the war and turned their thoughts to home. They were fortunate: Most of the North's cities and countryside had been spared the destruction of war, and most soldiers returned to homes that looked exactly as they remembered them. The northern economy had emerged from the war stronger than ever. All in all, life for most Northerners quickly returned to normal. And, as they heard stories of the terrible poverty and hardship in the South, many Northerners found it hard to stay angry at their former enemies.

Still, Yankee feelings against the defeated Confederacy ran hot in the first months after the war. The southern states had started the conflict in the first place by pulling out of the Union, Northerners reasoned. Rebel soldiers had killed or disabled hundreds of thousands of the North's young men. The war had cost the country millions of dollars and disrupted the lives of all northern men, women, and children.

There were those who thought that the men who led the rebels should pay with their lives. General John A. Dix of New York recommended that at least a few Confederate leaders "be tried and executed for treason." A farmer from Illinois wanted to take "all of the rebel officers and slaveholders" and "hang all of them five hundred feet high."

Decisions about punishing former rebels and readmitting the South to the Union were up to the U.S. Congress and Andrew Johnson, who became president after Abraham Lincoln was assassinated on April 14, 1865. A Democrat from Tennessee and a vocal Union supporter, Johnson had been chosen as vice president during the war to help convince northern Democrats to vote for Lincoln, who was a Republican.

Johnson's loyalty to the Union did not stem from anti-slavery feelings—he had owned five slaves before the war and was deeply racist. Rather, it grew out of his loathing for the southern planter aristocracy. A former tailor whose wife had taught him to read and write, Johnson had worked his way up from poverty to become a prosperous landowner and elected official—first as a state legislator, then as a member of Congress and governor of Tennessee. He could not forgive planters for leading lives of wealth and ease and for looking down on self-made men.

Johnson saw himself as representing the interests of non-slaveholding southern whites—the small farmers and craftsmen who made up two-thirds of the South's white population but whose interests the powerful politicians always

President Andrew Johnson led the country during the first three years after the Civil War. A Democrat, Johnson supported the return of white rule to the South and saw no need to protect or expand the rights of freed slaves.

seemed to overlook. Although non-slaveholders had made up the bulk of the Confederate Army, Johnson did not hold them responsible for the war or see any reason to deal with them harshly. On May 29, 1865, Johnson offered general "amnesty and restitution of property, except slaves," to most Confederates, as long as they took an oath of allegiance to the Union and supported the emancipation of slaves.

On the other hand, Johnson pledged to show no mercy toward those who had held high positions in the Confederate government or army. He considered them traitors who had incited others to take up arms against the Union. "Treason is a crime and must be made odious," Johnson said. "Traitors must be impoverished . . . They must not only be punished, but their social power must be destroyed."

Northerners were pleased by this tough talk. Many wanted Johnson to prosecute powerful Confederates for treason and to strip them of their land, their vote, and their power. The northern public also supported his decision to keep a two-hundred-thousand-man military force in the South to maintain law and order.

But President Johnson never carried through on his pledge to punish and impoverish the southern "traitors." He did exclude from the general amnesty high-ranking Confederate officials, military officers, and anyone who had owned property worth more than twenty thousand dollars before the war. But he gave them the option of applying to him in person for a pardon.

One by one, these rich and powerful men—or sometimes their elegant wives—appeared before Johnson humble and contrite, admitting their mistakes, and begging forgiveness. Satisfied to see the planters groveling, President Johnson granted pardons to nearly everyone who asked.

Whether they swore allegiance to the Union in their hometowns or in the presence of Andrew Johnson, few former Confederates believed the words they spoke. They held up their right hands and swore undying loyalty to the United States because that was the only way they could recover their rights and property, large chunks of which the Union had seized during the war.

Writing in her diary on July 28, 1865, Catherine Ann Devereux Edmondston of South Carolina noted with disgust that her brother had "asked & received pardon at the hand of his high mightiness

Andy Johnson for the crime of being worth more than $20,000." Edmondston derived some satisfaction from knowing that neither her brother, nor her father, nor her husband considered the oath binding. "Not one person whom I have heard speak of it but laughs at and repudiates every obligation it imposes," she said.

During the spring and summer of 1865, President Johnson chose temporary governors to run seven southern states until new constitutions could be written and new state governments elected. Johnson allowed the four other states that had left the Union—Arkansas, Louisiana, Tennessee, and Virginia—to continue operating under governments established by President Lincoln before he was killed. These governments had declared their loyalty to the Union before the end of the war and had taken steps to free slaves in their states.

New, all-white governments were soon elected in every southern state. Johnson's leniency toward former Confederates made it possible for many of the very same men who had held power before and during the Civil War to secure influential positions in these

Many Northerners wanted President Johnson to punish Southerners for starting the Civil War. They were disappointed when he offered quick amnesty to nearly every former rebel who would recite an oath of allegiance to the United States.

RESTORATION.

President Johnson's Amnesty Proclamation.

Restoration to Rights of Property Except in Slaves.

An Oath of Loyalty as a Condition Precedent.

Legality of Confiscation Proceedings Recognized.

Exception of Certain Offenders from this Amnesty.

By These Special Applications for Pardon May be Made.

Reorganization in North Carolina.

Appointment of a Provisional Governor.

A State Convention to be Chosen by Loyal Citizens.

The Machinery of the Federal Government to be Put in Operation.

AMNESTY PROCLAMATION.

governments. Although they had to abolish slavery and renounce secession, the state legislatures were not required to include black men in their new governments, and none did. Nor did any of the southern states adopt laws allowing former slaves to vote. "This is a white man's government, and intended for white men only," said the governor of South Carolina, expressing the sentiments of his fellow governors.

The new governments acted quickly to restrict the freedom of former slaves. They passed a series of harsh laws called Black Codes that limited freedmen and women to working as field hands or domestic servants. Many former rebels, emboldened by their return to power, began to commit brutal acts of violence against freed slaves and white Unionists. News of these events distressed and offended many Northerners. They did not think it right that former Confederates, who had put the nation through four years of hell, should be able to run the South however they pleased.

The stage was set for a fierce political battle. On one side were the "Radical" Republicans, who believed that the South should not be allowed back into the Union until it granted freedmen full political and civil rights. On the other side were those, including President Andrew Johnson, who favored denying such rights to black Americans and keeping all control in white hands. This battle nearly cost Johnson his presidency. It also kept alive the bitter feelings between North and South.

At the heart of the conflict was the fate of the four million freed slaves who, after a lifetime of bondage, were about to begin life as free men and women. Everyone in the South had their own worries and expectations about what that freedom would mean. Plantation owners were convinced that former slaves, whom they considered naturally lazy, would not work without the threat of whippings and other punishments. To make the fields of the South productive again—and to regain their own lost wealth—planters believed they should be allowed to reassert as much of the old control over their former slaves as possible.

Most small farmers hoped only to be able to restore their farms and their lives. But they preferred to do so without the meddling of Yankees, and they were nervous at the prospect of freed slaves demanding the same rights as white citizens.

Many planters refused to accept that freed slaves could no longer be bought and sold like farm animals. Here, a man is trying to sell his former slave, who owes him money.

Northerners wanted the South to start producing the cotton and other raw materials their factories depended upon—which meant getting freedmen and women back to work on the plantations as soon as possible.

But the overriding desire of former slaves was to buy or rent a piece of land and work for themselves, free of white supervision. They also wanted the chance to worship where they pleased and to educate themselves and their children. And they wanted the right

◆ Lines Drawn in Blood ◆

A great deal of the turbulence that rocked America during Reconstruction can be traced to differences between the nation's two main political parties: the Democrats and the Republicans.

The Republican party, which was founded in the North, was less than ten years old when the Civil War began. Abraham Lincoln was the first Republican president. The party was begun by people who believed that a strong national government was necessary to build the economy and protect the rights of individual Americans. In times of crisis, such as the Civil War and Reconstruction, Republicans felt that the federal government had the right and responsibility to assert its authority over state governments, whether the states liked it or not.

Republicans, including President Lincoln, were determined to force the renegade southern states back into the Union—on northern terms.

to vote, so they would be represented in the governments—local, state, and federal—that made decisions affecting their lives.

Homes, farms, cities, railroads, and bridges had been destroyed during the Civil War. Rebuilding them was a daunting task. But it was simple compared with the real challenge of Reconstruction— trying to rebuild the economic and personal relationship between two regions and two races with very different ideas of what life in post-Civil War America should be like.

Democrats, on the other hand, were firmly convinced that the federal government should be small, that it should have limited power, and that it should leave the states free to run their own affairs.

The spread of slavery was the issue over which the two parties clashed most bitterly— and which sparked the Civil War. Before the war, the South was solidly Democratic, and rich slaveholders were among the party's most powerful members. It was the Democrats in the South, supported by northern Democrats, who led efforts to expand slavery into the new states forming in the West. And when the Republican-controlled federal government refused to allow this expansion of slavery, southern Democrats led the movement to secede from the Union.

The South's defeat in the Civil War ensured that slavery would end and the Union would be preserved. It also resulted in the Democrats losing much of their power. They were associated with a losing cause and had no hope of winning the support of the four million freed slaves, who were loyal to the Republican party that had freed them. When former slaves won the right to vote, they elected Republicans to local, state, and national offices throughout the South, helping to make the Republican party the strongest in the region.

White Democrats in the South—or conservatives, as they began to call themselves after the war—fiercely resented being governed by Republicans. They sneeringly described them as "niggers, carpetbaggers, and scalawags," and vowed to return the South to Democratic rule.

Thus the battle lines of Reconstruction were drawn. On one side were the Republicans, who insisted that federal intervention in the South was necessary to protect the rights of freed slaves. On the other side were the Democrats, who would resist that intervention with so much determination and violence.

Former slaves greeted the news of freedom—and the Union soldiers who often delivered it—with great joy.

Two

◆ *A Place Called Freedom* ◆

*T*om Robinson looked up from the cow he was milking to see his master, Dave Robinson, walking toward him through the field, a piece of paper fluttering in his hand.

"Listen to me, Tom," the Texas plantation owner said. "Listen to what I read you."

Tom's curiosity turned to astonishment as Robinson began to read. The Civil War was over, he said, and Tom and every other slave was free. Convinced his master was playing a joke on him, Tom ran up to the house to ask Mrs. Robinson, who confirmed her husband's words.

Sold away from his mother in North Carolina when he was only ten years old, and sold twice more before he was fifteen, Tom had spent his entire life in slavery. Despite assurances from the Robinsons that he was free, Tom was still skeptical. "I just couldn't take it all in," he recalled. "I couldn't believe we was all free alike."

He decided to go see the Smiths, a black family that lived nearby, to "find out if they was free too." Out of a lifetime of habit, Tom asked Mrs. Robinson for permission to leave the plantation. "Don't you understand?" Tom remembered her saying. "You're free. You don't have to ask me what you can do."

More slaves learned they were free from Yankee soldiers passing through plantations or towns than from their owners. But however the news reached them, most slaves greeted the prospect of freedom with joy. "We was dancin' and prancin' an' yellin' wid a big barn fir [bonfire] jus' ablazin'," recalled Anne Harris, a former slave from Petersburg, Virginia. "Purty soon ev'ybody fo' miles around was singin' freedom songs. One went like dis:

I's free, I's free, I's free at las'!
Thank God A'mighty, I's free at las'!"

The moment Louise Bowes Rose heard the news, she ran to tell her father, who was filling water jugs from a creek on the plantation where they lived. "He jumped right in de water up to his neck," Rose remembered. "He was so happy he jus' kep' on scoopin' up han'fulls of water an dumpin' it on his haid an' yellin', 'I'se free, I'se free! I'se free!'"

No longer would black Americans suffer the "awfulness," as one former slave described it, "of . . . belongin' to folks what own you, soul an' body." No longer would husband and wife have to live with the terrible fear that one of them—or one of their children—would be sold to another owner far away.

For the first time in their lives, former slaves could go to sleep knowing they would not be awakened before dawn by a blast from the overseer's horn, calling them to another long day in the fields. They could do their work without the fear of being lashed repeatedly with a bullwhip for breaking the slightest rule. No more would they have to sneak off to the woods to a "brush arbor" (a makeshift church constructed of four tree saplings, stuck in the ground, with leaves and brush piled on top and against the sides) to worship in their own way. No longer would they have to muffle the sounds of their "talk wid Jesus" by praying or singing into a large iron pot.

None of the early sensations of freedom was more exhilarating than being able to leave the plantation without the fear of being arrested by plantation overseers or patrollers, usually poor whites hired by landowners to watch for runaway slaves.

"Right off, colored folks started on the move," recalled ex-slave Felix Haywood. "They seemed to want to get closer to freedom, so they'd know what it wuz—like it wuz a place or a city." For some it was enough to walk to a neighboring plantation. Others, especially skilled craftsmen, set off for nearby cities and towns in the hopes of finding well-paying jobs. A few traveled north or west seeking work in expanding industries such as mining, ranching, and farming, or on the fast-growing network of railroads.

Thousands set out in search of loved ones—husbands, wives, children, and siblings—whose owners had sold them away from their families. The results of these searches were usually disappointing. Sometimes former slaves managed to track down their spouses only

This freedman has loaded his family and their few belongings into a cart for the journey from the plantation where they toiled as slaves. Note the pitiful condition of the ox—the few farm animals left alive in the South at the end of the war were usually half-dead from starvation and neglect.

> **INFORMATION WANTED,**
>
> OF Caroline Dodson, who was sold from Nashville, Nov. 1st, 1862, by James Lumsden to Warwick (a trader then in human beings), who carried her to Atlanta, Georgia, and she was last heard of in the sale pen of Robert Clarke (human trader in that place), from which she was sold. Any information of her whereabouts will be thankfully received and rewarded by her mother.
>
> LUCINDA LOWERY,
> Nashville.

Many freedmen and women spent years searching for lost mothers, fathers, daughters, and sons. They hoped against hope that notices such as this one, which ran in the *Colored Tennessean*, would lead to a reunion with loved ones.

to find they had remarried or died during the long separation. Others searched for years, even decades, without finding a trace of their relatives.

The odds were against finding lost family members. Few slave traders kept written records, and former slaves had to rely on whatever scraps of information they could find to guide their search. Often they traveled to the city or town where the family member had last been seen and inquired at black churches and Union military headquarters. In giving descriptions, they had to draw on memories of what their spouses or children—now adults—had looked like years before.

For all the searches that ended in heartbreak, there was also the occasional miracle, such as the one that happened to Nancy White of Richmond, Virginia. Long before the Civil War, when her son Garland was a small boy, he had been bought by Robert Toombs, a Georgia lawyer who wanted a personal servant.

For years she heard nothing. Then, during the war, Mrs. White happened to see Toombs (who had joined the Confederate Army) in Richmond with his unit. She approached him and asked what had become of her son. "He ran off from me at Washington and went to Canada," the lawyer told her. "I have since learned that he is living somewhere in the state of Ohio." There the trail went cold.

In April 1865, with the war nearly over, Mrs. White was among the thousands of freed slaves thronging the streets of Richmond to watch victorious Union troops, led by several black regiments, march through the city. Discovering that some of the units were from the North, Mrs. White pushed through to the front of the dense crowd and asked every soldier she could if he knew her son Garland. By a stroke of luck, one soldier she asked had heard of a Garland H. White; he was a chaplain with the Twenty-eighth U.S. Colored Infantry, an Indiana regiment.

The soldier told the old woman to wait and went in search of White. When he returned with the chaplain, Mrs. White asked the man a series of questions:

"What is your name, sir?"

"My name is Garland H. White."

"What was your mother's name?"

"Nancy."

"Where was you sold from?"

"From this city."

"What was the name of the man who bought you?"

"Robert Toombs."

"Where did he live?"

"In the state of Georgia."

"Where did you leave him?"

"At Washington."

"Where did you then go?"

"To Canada."

"Where do you now live?"

"In Ohio."

At that the old woman burst into tears. "This is your mother, Garland, whom you are now talking to, who has spent twenty years of grief about her son."

Once the initial jubilation of being free and reuniting with loved ones had passed, ex-slaves' thoughts turned to the practical aspects of living as free men and women. Some, especially older people and widows with children, worried about where they would live, and how they would feed and clothe their families. Before freedom, their owners had taken care of such needs.

Freedman Thomas Cole remembers that "de first few years it was awful hard to gets adjusted to de new life dat was in front of dem. All de slaves knew how to do hard work, for dey was taught dat from de time dey was big enough to work till they died. . . . But dere was very few dat was taught or knows anything 'bout how to find a job er how to depend on demselves for a livin'.

But a few years of scrapin' and scratchin' for deir own food, it wasn't so hard."

The dream of most freed slaves was to buy—or at least rent— a piece of land on which they could build a home, grow crops, and be their own boss. They were well aware that without land, the chief source of wealth and power in the agricultural South, they were likely to remain dependent upon whites for their livelihoods. Also, owning land provided emotional security: for the first time in their lives, former slaves would have something no one could take away from them, and that they could pass on to their children.

"What's de use of being free if you don't own land enough to be buried in?" one old black man asked northern journalist Whitelaw Reid, who traveled through the South for an entire year after the war. "Might juss as well stay slave all yo' days."

Freedmen's hopes were lifted by rumors that the federal government planned to give them "forty acres and a mule" to help them get started. The rumors began circulating in 1863, when the Union government allowed black refugees to farm land abandoned by Confederates who had fled Union-occupied territory and land confiscated from southern planters who had failed to pay their federal taxes.

Hopes grew in January 1865, when a special government order set aside coastal islands and other land in South Carolina, Georgia, and Florida for farming by former slaves. Providing the refugees with land gave the Union Army a way to settle the thousands of slaves who had left their plantations and followed Union General William Tecumseh Sherman and his armies on their march through the South. "Each family," the order declared, "shall have a plot of not more than forty acres of tillable ground." By June, more than ten thousand freedmen and women were farming close to five hundred thousand acres. Some rented and some eventually bought the land they worked.

Republican Congressman Thaddeus Stevens and others who supported equality for freed slaves argued in favor of expanding this policy. They proposed that the federal government divide up the land of rich Confederates and give a forty-acre parcel to *every* adult freedman. Such a policy, they reasoned, would punish disloyal slaveholders and reward former slaves, who had worked all their lives without pay and had been loyal to—and in many cases fought for—the Union.

This rundown cabin may not look like much, but it was more than these freed slaves had ever had in their lives.

This idea proved too radical for most members of Congress. They believed that the rebels had been punished enough by losing the war and their slaves, and should not have to lose their land as well. Former slaves would have to obtain land the same way poor white Northerners did—by earning the money to buy it.

Freed slaves who had settled on a plot of confiscated or abandoned land during the war received a bitter shock when the property's original owners—pardoned by President Andrew Johnson—returned to claim it. Freedmen were given two choices: stay on the land and work for wages, or leave. Many refused to do either. But when they resisted, sometimes violently, efforts to throw them off land they now considered their own, the federal government intervened on the side of the ex-Confederates.

The dream of owning land did come true for some freed slaves. Sometimes, several black soldiers pooled money they had earned during the war and bought an entire plantation on which several families settled. In rare cases, generous plantation owners left their former slaves a piece of land in their will.

◆ "Why Do You Take Away Our Lands?" ◆

The rumor raced among the black families on Edisto Island— the federal government was taking their land away!

It was the fall of 1865, and nearly six hundred former slave families were farming thousands of acres on Edisto Island, one of the South Carolina Sea Islands. Each family had been settled on a forty-acre plot under General William Tecumseh Sherman's order of January 1865, with the understanding that they could eventually buy the land.

Now, they had heard that General O. O. Howard, the director of the Freedmen's Bureau, was coming to strip them of their farms. The news angered and frightened the settlers. They knew that the land's original owners—white men who had supported the Confederacy and abandoned their

plantations when the Union Army approached—wanted their property back. But they also knew that the Freedmen's Bureau had been set up in part to protect the rights of freed slaves. Would the government now go back on its promise to the freedmen? Would they lose the land they had so recently gained?

Black settlers' worst fears were confirmed at a meeting with Howard on October 19. President Johnson had pardoned the rebel planters, Howard told the assembled families, and agreed to restore their property. "Why, General Howard, why do you take away our lands?" one man asked. "You take them from us who have always been true . . . to the Government! You give them to our all-time enemies! That is not right!"

The freedmen could remain

Former slaves who could not afford to buy land sometimes managed to save enough money to rent. Among them was Tom Robinson, who worked for a plantation owner for a year or two after the war, saving every penny he could. "Pretty soon I had me enough that I could rent," he recalled with pride. "I always raised enough to eat for us and the stock—and then some cotton for a cash crop." Robinson worked as a farmer for the rest of his life and always managed to produce enough to support his large family.

Even when freedmen had money, white landowners usually were reluctant to sell or rent land to them. Northern journalist Whitelaw

on the land, Howard assured them; all they had to do was sign a contract to work for the land's "legal" owners. He advised them to lay aside their bitter feelings toward the planters—in many cases the freedmen's old masters—and negotiate the best terms they could for their labor.

Freed slaves left the meeting feeling betrayed. Most vowed "never to make contracts with, or work for, their former owners." The settlers organized rallies and sent letters of protest to General Howard and President Johnson.

"You ask us to forgive the land owners of our Island," a committee of three freedmen wrote to General Howard. "You only lost your right arm [i]n the war and might forgive them. The man who tied me to a tree & gave me 39 lashes & who stripped and flogged my mother & sister . . . that man, I cannot well forgive."

To President Johnson, the petitioners wrote that they would gladly pay the government for the land, if only given the chance. They asked the president to guarantee that every freed slave could buy a piece of land and "have a home if it be but a few acres."

These heartfelt pleas had no effect. Some families left the island rather than hire out to the hated landowners. Some eventually signed contracts, although with great reluctance. But many stood firm, refusing either to sign a labor contract or leave. Agents of the Freedmen's Bureau warned the holdouts that if they continued to resist they would be considered trespassers—and forcibly evicted by Union soldiers.

Despite the threats, many settlers stayed put. True to its word, in February and early March the U.S. government sent in federal troops, who forced the holdouts off the plantations.

Reid noted that in much of the Mississippi Valley "the feeling against any ownership of the soil by the Negroes is so strong that the man who should sell small tracts to them would be in actual personal danger. Every effort will be made to prevent Negroes from acquiring lands; and even the renting of small tracts to them is held to be unpatriotic and unworthy of good citizens."

When former slaves did find someone willing to sell or rent land to them, white planters sometimes tried to sabotage their efforts to live independently. Joe Bright, who had been free before the war, leased forty acres in Duplin County, North Carolina, from a white man. The two worked out an arrangement under which Bright would keep two-thirds of the crop and give the landowner one-third as rent. Bright brought his wife and children, formerly slaves in a neighboring county, to live with him.

Local planters were indignant at the thought of a black man farming on his own, rather than working for wages under a white planter. Knowing Bright could not make the farm a success without the labor of his six children (aged twelve to eighteen), they conspired to take the children away.

The planters convinced local authorities that Bright did not make a good enough living to support his children and that the state should apprentice all six to them. Laws in many southern states allowed planters to "apprentice" black orphans and children whose parents could not support them until they reached adulthood. Not only did this plan ensure the ruin of Joe Bright, it had the added advantage of providing the planters with six strong young field hands at no cost. The children would become virtual slaves.

Armed with an official order, three white men forcibly took Bright's children "from the corn field and plow and carried them off to their house." Bright immediately lodged a protest with the Union officer overseeing his county. "I am a mason and Plaster[er]," Bright wrote to the officer, "and can bring plenty of wittness that I am perfectly eable to Suport my family by my hard labor and work and would do right well if people . . . would not interfere with my family matters."

The Union officer agreed with Joe Bright and helped him to recover his children.

Freed slaves recognized that, like obtaining land, knowing how to read and write was vital to their struggle to take control of their lives. During slavery, most owners severely punished slaves who tried to educate themselves. "Us was whooped if us even looked into a book," said Louis Meadows, a former slave from Alabama. The few slaves who did learn their "letters" (in many cases from the children of their owners, with whom they were allowed to play when young) kept their ability a careful secret.

During the Civil War, northern missionaries and representatives of freedmen's aid societies had traveled south to organize schools for former slaves in Union-held territory. After the war, these Northerners were joined by freedmen and women. Schools sprang up everywhere—in old slave quarters, abandoned buildings, and church basements.

Freed slaves were determined to educate themselves and their children. By 1867, nearly every county in the South had at least one school where black students of all ages were taught.

The first school former slave Maggie Black attended was no more than four posts stuck in the ground, with a ceiling of logs covered by brush; pupils sat on a log and their teacher stood on a box. The Bible and Webster's *Dictionary* were often the only schoolbooks available.

Children walked as far as five or ten miles each way to attend school. Classes were frequently held at night since nearly everyone, even children, had to work during the day. Freed slaves ranging in age from seven to seventy-five crowded into the classrooms.

◆ The War Against Teachers ◆

After the war, Maria Waterbury traveled with another white missionary from Chicago to Tennessee to set up a school for former slaves. The two women were close to the end of their arduous journey by train, steamboat, mule-drawn cart, covered wagon, and foot when they were forced by rain and impassable roads to stop for the night only six miles from their destination. The house that had been recommended to them had no room, so the missionaries tried the Armstrong sisters just down the road. The sisters, however, had heard of the proposed school and wanted nothing to do with the missionaries.

"You are *ladies*," one of the sisters told the exhausted travelers, "and before I'd teach a nigger school, I'd beg my bread from door to door. No you can't come into our house . . . *Nigger teacher*, indeed! As though *we* would disgrace ourselves having them in our house!"

When Waterbury and her friend finally reached the community where they were to teach, their employer, a planter, was happy to see them. He hoped that setting up a school would please his former slaves and encourage them to stay and work on his plantation. But the planter's white neighbors were so hostile that he had to move the teachers into his own house, for fear the building where they were to live and teach would be torched.

"The war against us has begun," Maria Waterbury observed soon after her arrival, "and we are threatened with many things." The teachers spent Christmas shut up in the planter's house, afraid to venture outside,

"It was a whole race trying to go to school," recalled Booker T. Washington, a former slave whose education started after the Civil War and who became America's foremost black educator. "Few were too young and none were too old to make the attempt to learn," said Washington.

Some of those who learned to read and write became teachers themselves. After she was freed, Mary Jane Wilson's chief desire was to teach. Her father, who was one of the first black landowners in Portsmouth, Virginia, fully supported her desire to get an education.

COPY OF A KU-KLUX LETTER.

Scipio.

Miss W———

We send you a picture of the way we treated a Yankee school ma'am in this county last year. Beware lest you shear the same fate.

Regulaters.

and with freedmen on constant guard.

Frightened but determined, the women opened their school in an old building where white students had studied during slave times; now, said Waterbury, it was "a harbor for rats by day, and dogs by night." The threats against them escalated. One day, the teachers received a picture of a white woman tied to a tree, a man standing on each side of her, one holding "an overseer's whip, laying strokes on her back." Beneath the picture was written, "This is the way we serve northern *nigger teachers*. Beware! lest you share the same fate."

The two missionaries survived their first year of teaching unharmed and, after spending the summer back in Chicago, returned to teach for six more years.

Maria Waterbury received a chilling message similar to this one.

Until work was completed on Portsmouth's new black secondary school, Wilson attended a makeshift school in a church. She finished her education at the recently opened Hampton Institute, at that time a training school for teachers and farmers. Soon after graduating in 1874, Wilson opened a school in the home her father had built for his family. "After two years my class grew so fast and large that my father built a school for me in our back yard," she recalled. "I had as many as seventy-five pupils at one time. Many of them became teachers."

Southern whites were divided about the value of educating former slaves. Many believed blacks were incapable of learning and that trying to teach them was a waste of time. "You might as well try to teach your horse or mule to read, as to teach these niggers," one white woman advised a teacher. Some plantation owners provided their employees with basic education, in the belief that it would make them better workers. Other white conservatives thought that educating former slaves was dangerous. What if learning how to read and write gave them the notion that they were as good as white people and deserved the same rights and privileges?

Freedmen's schools and the Northerners who came to teach in them were regarded with suspicion and hostility. "The citizens have opposed by all means in their power the continuance of the great work of education in the country parishes," reported the New Orleans *Tribune* in September

Julia Hayden, a seventeen-year-old teacher at a freedmen's school in Tennessee, was murdered by white vigilantes. Many white Southerners were enraged by efforts to help freed slaves learn to read and write.

1866. "They have refused to rent buildings for school purposes and to board the teachers. They have whipped Mr. LeBlanc at Point Coupee; dangerously stabbed in the back Mr. Burnham at Monroe; and beaten almost to death Mr. Ruby at Jackson." Many schools were burned to the ground.

White Southerners also watched with alarm the growing number and influence of black churches. No institution proved more important in the transition from slavery to freedom than the church. During slavery, the only choice for black families who wanted to worship formally was to attend white churches, where they were seated in the back or in second-floor galleries. After the war, white churches continued to segregate the two races. Thousands of black families decided to form their own congregations and hire their own preachers. In South Carolina in 1861, some forty-two thousand black Methodists worshipped in white churches; by the 1870s, only six hundred did.

The first new building erected in Charleston, South Carolina, after the war was a black church; by 1866, the city boasted eleven such churches. Until the buildings were completed, former slaves worshipped wherever they could find space. In Atlanta, members of the First Baptist Church held services in a railroad boxcar.

A white mob burns a freedmen's school in Memphis, Tennessee.

Churches quickly became the most important institutions in black communities throughout the South. Besides being places of worship, they also acted as schoolhouses and the sites of social events and political gatherings. Ministers, often among the only people in a community who could read and write, were widely respected and frequently became political as well as spiritual leaders. Most preached not just the gospel but also voting rights, education, and equal protection under the law. Ministers also taught school and held important local, state, and federal offices.

White conservatives were convinced that activist black preachers would encourage rebellious and vengeful behavior by former slaves. Ministers were beaten, and their churches burned, in a futile attempt to stop them from preaching politics.

White Southerners' hostility toward black churches and schools underscored how hard it was for them to think of former slaves as independent men and women with the same rights as white citizens. The adoption of the Thirteenth Amendment to the Constitution in December 1865 had officially outlawed slavery in the United States. But as George King remembered his former owner telling him, the fact that slaves were free "don't mean we is white, and it don't mean we is equal—just equal for to work and earn our own living and not depend on him for no more eats and clothes."

Sidney Andrews, a white journalist from the North, traveled through South Carolina, North Carolina, and Georgia for several months after the end of the war, talking with hundreds of former slaves and Confederates. He observed that "The whites seem wholly unable to comprehend that freedom for the Negro means the same thing as freedom for them . . . they appear to believe that they still have the right to exercise over him the old control."

The new all-white state legislatures elected in the post-war South moved quickly to hem in the freed slaves. Their first step was to pass Black Codes, a series of laws that created rules by which freedmen and women were supposed to live. Some of these laws expanded freedmen's rights, permitting them to own and sell property (personal property only in Mississippi), make legal contracts, legally marry, and testify in court (although only in cases where black citizens alone were involved).

But the codes also denied black citizens the right to serve on

Now that they were free, black Southerners could marry legally. Before, although they had their own wedding ceremonies and traditions, slaves' marriages were not considered legal.

juries, forbade whites and blacks to marry one another, and gave courts the authority to punish blacks more severely than whites for the same crime. The laws imposed stiff penalties on former slaves who assumed that freedom gave them the right to mingle with whites as equals. The Florida Black Codes stated that "any person of color . . . who shall intrude himself into any religious or other public assembly of white persons or into any railroad car or other vehicle set apart for the accommodation of white persons shall stand in the pillory [a wooden board with holes for the head and arms] . . . for one hour and then [be] whipped with thirty-nine lashes on the bare back."

Offensive as they were, these restrictions were minor compared with the laws at the heart of every southern state's Black Codes—laws designed to put freedmen and women back to work on plantations under the absolute control of whites. In South Carolina, which passed one of the harshest codes, freed slaves could work only as field hands or servants unless they obtained a special license and paid a steep fee. Servants were required to work from sunup to sundown and could be whipped "moderately."

Former slaves who signed a contract could not leave the plantation or have visitors without permission from their employer. Any former slave found without work could be charged with vagrancy and sentenced to up to twelve months of hard labor on a white-owned farm.

News of these harsh new laws soon reached the North, where many citizens, including Democrats, reacted angrily. Most Northerners, though hardly free of racial prejudice, believed that former slaves should be guaranteed basic legal protections, and be free to work and live as they chose without interference from whites. The Black Codes struck many Northerners as a shameless attempt by southern lawmakers to "restore all of slavery but its name" and, as such, an insult to the Union victory in the Civil War. The Chicago *Tribune* issued a warning to "the white men of Mississippi" in an editorial on December 1, 1865: "The men of the North will convert the state of Mississippi into a frog pond before they will allow any such laws to disgrace one foot of soil in which the bones of our soldiers sleep and over which the flag of freedom waves."

Federal lawmakers who had fought for rights for black Americans vowed to keep southern states out of the Union until they expanded the rights of freedmen and women. Freed slaves throughout the South sent petitions to Congress and their state governments demanding repeal of the Black Codes. In South Carolina and Mississippi, they organized political conventions to develop strategies for combating the new laws.

SEC. 2. *Be it further enacted*, That all freed-men, free Negroes and mulattoes in this State, over the age of eighteen years, found on the second Monday in January, 1866, or thereafter, without lawful employment or business, or found unlawfully assembling themselves together, either in the day or night time, and all white persons so assembling themselves with freedmen, free Negroes or mulat-toes, or usually associating with freedmen, free Negroes or mulattoes . . . shall be deemed vagrants, and on conviction thereof shall be fined in a sum not exceeding, in the case of a freedman, free Ne-gro, or mulatto, fifty dollars, and a white man two hundred dollars, and imprisoned, at the discretion of the court, the free Negro not exceeding ten days, and the white man not exceeding six months.

This section of the Mississippi Black Codes ordered that all black men must have jobs by the second Monday of January 1866, or risk imprisonment and a fine of fifty dollars.

Acting under orders from high-level federal officials, Union soldiers stationed in the South prevented white Southerners from enforcing the worst provisions of the Black Codes. But that alone was not enough to guarantee real improvements in the lives of freed slaves.

By the fall of 1865, many freedmen and women were discouraged in their attempts to find relatives, to make a living in the impoverished towns and cities of the South, and to buy or rent land. They felt they had no choice but to return to the plantations they had left months before with so much hope, and hire themselves out to their former owners. At least now they would be free laborers, working for a fair wage. Or so they thought.

After the war, the Paterson Iron Company in New Jersey, like other factories in the North, quickly switched from producing cannonballs to making parts for railroads and steamboats.

THREE

• *"Times Is Powerful Hard"* •

W hen northern journalist J. T. Trowbridge set out on a journey through the post-Civil War South in June 1865, he left behind a booming economy. The demand for weapons and ammunition during the war had boosted the output of factories producing iron, steel, and machine tools in the North. Farm production had also increased, both to make up for the loss of southern commodities and to provide enough grain, meat, and cotton to feed and clothe the Union Army.

Now that the war was over, the North could pour most of its money into further expansion and new technology, instead of spending every dollar on rebuilding, as the South was forced to do. Northern farms and factories continued to churn out goods, producing iron for railroad tracks, fabric for clothing, and food for the region's growing population. As railroad construction moved west of the Mississippi River, new opportunities were opening up in lumbering, mining, farming, and ranching. Jobs were plentiful, and the future looked bright.

Starkly different conditions greeted Trowbridge as he traveled through the southern states of Alabama, Florida, Georgia, Louisiana, Mississippi, North Carolina, South Carolina, and Virginia. Destruction and poverty were everywhere. In Atlanta, which had been burned to the ground during the war, he found "ruins and rubbish, mud and mortar and misery. The burnt streets were rapidly rebuilding; but in the meanwhile hundreds of the inhabitants, white and black, rendered homeless by the destruction of the city, were living in wretched hovels."

The war had left many of Atlanta's residents with "nothing but the rags on their back," said Trowbridge, and hundreds were forced to beg for food. One former slave told the journalist she had lost her home after her husband was killed fighting for the Union Army. Now, like many other impoverished blacks, she lived in a makeshift hut constructed of old boards and "covered entirely with ragged fragments of tin-roofing from the burnt government and railroad buildings."

The widow supported her six children by washing the clothes and linens of white families. "Sometimes I gits along tolerable; sometimes right slim," she told Trowbridge, "but that's the way with everybody—times is powerful hard right now."

The families of rebel soldiers, too, suffered the "extremes of want," said Trowbridge. Their men had been paid in Confederate dollars, which now had no value. Poor diets, crowded living conditions, and the lack of pure drinking water led to the rapid spread of infectious diseases such as smallpox and yellow fever. "As at nearly every other town of any note in the South which I visited," Trowbridge wrote, "the smallpox was raging at Atlanta, chiefly among the blacks, and the suffering poor whites."

Apart from the federal troops still stationed in the South, the only source of help available to the thousands of men, women, and children of both races left penniless by the war was the Bureau of Refugees, Freedmen and Abandoned Lands, known as the Freedmen's Bureau. The federal government created the bureau in March 1865 to distribute food, clothing, and fuel to people in need, and to help freed slaves make the transition to freedom. Offices were set up throughout the South and, in the early days, staffed mostly by Union soldiers.

Bureau agents distributed millions of "rations"—usually consisting of a week's worth of corn meal or flour, sometimes with sugar, rice, tea, and other items—to those who were poor, old, orphaned, sick, or without work. "In that period of transition," noted Trowbridge, people would have "perished in masses without such aid."

Even members of the planter class suffered after the war, Trowbridge reported, although they rarely went without food or shelter. "Their fences destroyed, buildings burned, farming implements worn out, horses, mules, and other stock consumed by both armies, investments in Confederate bonds worthless, bank-stock gone, without money, or anything to exchange for money, they had often only their bare lands on which to commence life anew," he wrote.

Many planters who had lived in luxury before the war found themselves sleeping on the floor, using boxes and barrels for furniture,

Not all farmers in the South owned grand plantations. Many small farms were run by families who worked the land themselves, without slaves. These small farmers suffered greatly from the war, and thousands turned to the Freedmen's Bureau for food, clothing, and other necessities.

and spending their days fishing and hunting for their next meal. Women wore dresses made of calico and homespun cloth instead of silk and taffeta, and tallow candles replaced gas-powered lamps. Luxuries such as imported wine, oysters, and fine cuts of beef disappeared from their dinner tables.

Women whose every need had been met by slaves now had to learn to clean and cook and sew. Men whose only job had been to tell their slaves what to do were forced not only to go to work but to take orders from others. Writing in her diary in June 1865, Clarissa Adger Bowen of South Carolina described the fate of several former planters in her community. "Mr. Gaillard is a clerk on a small salary, the young Coffins are hauling brick . . . [and] Rutledge Holmes intends buying provisions, wagoning them down the country to sell so he can bring back articles needed up here."

Once the owners of a sizable estate in Louisiana, Confederate General Braxton Bragg and his wife, Elisa, found themselves "without a dollar at the close of our shameful and degrading contest." The couple spent nearly a year living in a former slave cabin while Bragg managed another man's plantation. He and his wife had "plenty to eat," Bragg wrote to a friend in April 1866, "and by moving about could find a dry spot when it rains."

What he really missed, General Bragg confided to his friend, was the kind of life he and his wife had led before the war— a life of "books, papers [and] society. . . . Not a human being has ever called to see us." He worried about having no money and no way to provide his "poor wife, raised in affluence & luxury," with the comforts she was used to. Life eventually improved for

Braxton Bragg, a former career soldier, left his sugar plantation and returned to duty as a Confederate general during the Civil War. When the Confederacy lost, Bragg found himself landless and penniless; he struggled for years to rebuild his life.

the Braggs, but only after they abandoned farming and the general accepted an appointment as Alabama's commissioner of public works.

Like Bragg, many southern planters were left with no choice but to sell or rent their land and go to work in towns or cities. Some took up a profession, such as banking or law; others set themselves up in business. A few, after struggling for a year or two to coax a profit out of their plantations, moved north, west, or even to Europe to make a new start. Still, thousands of planters remained on their land, doggedly working to rebuild their former wealth.

Planters all faced the same problem: where to find the credit to replace their livestock and machinery and to buy seed to plant new crops. Before the war, planters used the value of their slaves and land as a basis for buying or borrowing as much as they needed. But the war wiped out slavery and drastically reduced the worth of land in the South. Suddenly, credit was much harder for planters to obtain.

When they were approached by planters asking for a loan, local merchants faced a difficult choice. They could refuse credit to their old customers and risk making enemies of them, or extend credit and risk never being repaid. Many businesses were forced to operate on a cash-only basis or close. "Everybody wanted to buy and nobody had any money," explained an Alabama furniture dealer forced to shut down his business.

Planters, small farmers, business people, banks, churches, schools, charitable organizations—individuals and institutions at every level of southern society—were broke.

The scarcity of money and credit was a direct result of how the South financed its war effort—by persuading state governments, institutions, and individual citizens to buy government bonds and treasury notes. The Confederate government promised that once the war was won, everyone would be paid back, with interest. Most Southerners, confident the Confederacy would triumph and eager to help the cause, turned over their gold and silver, and sometimes their crops. Several European governments, too, loaned millions of dollars to the Confederacy.

But when the war was over, there was no money to pay back the huge debt. The defeat of the South meant that the paper money printed by both the Confederate government and southern state governments

The Confederate States of America printed this paper currency to finance the war.

during the war was absolutely worthless. At first, some Southerners even hoped the North would help them get back on their feet. Such help was only fair, they reasoned, since the North, after all, had ruined the southern economy by ending slavery.

One day in Virginia, Trowbridge overheard a well-dressed white woman grumble to a northern man, "You ought to do something for us, for you've took away our niggers." When the Northerner pointed out that the "South owed the loss of its slaves to its own folly," the woman was silent for a moment. But she quickly began to complain again that nothing was being done for her, although, Trowbridge noted, she was "obliged to confess that she owned the house she lived in, and another for which two colored families were paying rent."

Hopes that the North might ease the South's losses by paying its war debts or by compensating plantation owners for the loss of their slaves were soon dashed. In fact, the federal government demanded that the South pay a portion of the *northern* war debt. Shortly after the war ended, the government began taxing agricultural and other goods produced by the South, including cotton, to help the North pay off its loans. In Georgia alone, federal agents collected nearly twelve million dollars in cotton taxes between 1866 and 1868.

Landowners who did obtain the seed, livestock, and machinery they needed to make a new start—often by pledging a part of their crop—still had to find workers to sow and harvest their fields. The obvious choice was former slaves. But neither planters nor freedmen were prepared for how the end of slavery had changed their working relationship.

Agents of the Freedmen's Bureau had the difficult task of trying to represent the interests of former masters *and* former slaves in developing a new form of labor relations, one based on employers and employees, not slaveowners and slaves. Most Northerners

Tempers often flared between white and black Southerners. Union soldiers and agents of the Freedmen's Bureau tried to keep the peace whenever possible, as shown in this idealized image.

felt that the best way for former slaves to get used to the "free labor" system that operated in the North was for them to return to work on the plantations under contract. This was also the best way to restart the large-scale production of cotton, tobacco, sugar, and other vital raw materials needed for northern and European mills and factories.

Bureau agents relied on annual labor contracts to spell out what was expected of both planters and freedmen. In many parts of the South, planters had to submit their labor contracts to the local Freedmen's Bureau for approval. If the agent thought a contract was unfair in any way, he could tell the planter to revise it.

The principles of free labor were second nature to most agents of the Freedmen's Bureau, nearly all of whom had grown up in the North. Under a free labor system, the following rules applied: Employers owed workers a fair wage and fair treatment, but none of the other necessities of life; employers could not punish workers physically; employers had the right to fire workers who failed to do an adequate job. Employees, for their part, had the right to leave a job if they felt they were being treated unfairly.

Unlike the bureau agents, freedmen and planters were hearing about free labor for the first time, and neither group adapted quickly or easily to this new way of working. Former slaves had trouble adjusting to the fact that their employers would not feed, clothe, and house them as their owners had. Instead, freedmen would earn wages for their work—and it was up to them to use those wages to take care of themselves and their families.

Many freed people were disappointed to find that working and living conditions under wage labor did not differ much from slavery. Families often lived in the same cabins they had occupied as slaves and worked in gangs in the field, closely watched by white overseers.

Planters were no happier than freed slaves with the wage labor system. No longer could they rely on physical punishment—or the threat of it—to get the "best" out of their workers. They bitterly resented having to clear their labor arrangements through northern officials. And they disliked and frequently rebelled against having to pay for labor they had once commanded for free.

George A. Harmount, assistant superintendent of the Freedmen's

Raleigh N.C. July 1st 1865

CIRCULAR NO 1.

. . . A great social revolution is going on. The united wisdom of all classes will be required to guide it to a successful issue. The Negro has become free, but he has not become an object of indifference. His interests and those of the white man are the same. He cannot with safety be treated with neglect, or scorn, or cruelty. He is human, and is entitled to all the rights of a man. Withhold from the Freedmen fair wages for their labor, deny them a right to a fair hearing before courts of justice, discourage their efforts to accumulate property, and to acquire learning, and you will drive from the State its real wealth—its productive labor. On the other hand, give to the Freedmen that which is just and equal, give them all the facilities possible for improvement and education, and you will secure in the State its best supporters and its truest friends. The School House, the Spelling Book, and the Bible will be found better preservers of peace and good order than the revolver and bowie knife.

I invite the cooperation of Freedmen also. Without your help this Bureau can do but little for you. Your freedom imposes upon you new duties. Some of you have families; it is your duty to support them. Some of you have aged parents and relatives, to whom liberty has come too late; it is your duty to minister to their comfort. Some of you will meet with helpless orphans; it is your duty to supply to them, as far as you can, the places of their lost parents. It is your duty, in common with all men, to obey the laws of the land, to live honestly, uprightly, and in the fear of God. . . .

HDcS

E. Whittlesey

Circular No 1., Bureau of Refugees, Freedmen &c Hd. Qrs. Asst. Commissioner, State of N.C., 1 July 1865, vol. 28, General Orders & Circulars Issued, ser. 2457, NC Asst. Comr., RG 105 [A-10802].

This circular, written by an assistant commissioner of the Freedmen's Bureau, explains to former slaves and former slaveowners what their new rights and responsibilities are. Such circulars were posted in public places for all to read, or have read to them.

Bureau in Mobile, Alabama, sought advice from his superior on how to handle the numerous cases that "come before me every day of persons refusing to pay Negroes the wages agreed upon—and yet these contracts have been made in my office.

"The people here feel indignant that they are obliged to hire the Negroes they used to own," Harmount wrote, "and will by every possible means endeavour to evade the payment of wages due them."

Even though the Freedmen's Bureau issued guidelines forbidding such treatment, many planters continued to put sections in their contracts that permitted them to whip "disobedient" or "disrespectful" workers and to punish men who used "impudent, profane or

These former slaves are harvesting cotton in a gang in the fields, just as they did before they were freed.

In a painful reminder of their past, many freedmen and women who signed labor contracts wound up living in the same cabins they had occupied as slaves.

indecent language." Others drew up contracts that required freedmen to ask permission before leaving the plantation for any reason.

Such strict rules were absolutely necessary, planters argued. "We must be left to manage the nigger," the manager of a five-thousand-acre plantation in Louisiana told Trowbridge. "He can't be made to work without force. . . . My theory is, feed 'em well, clothe 'em well, and then, if they won't work, whip 'em well!"

Freedmen's Bureau agents frequently refused to approve contracts that gave planters too much control. Agents also fought attempts by planters to require laborers to carry passes whenever they left the plantation, just as they had during slavery.

Even in contracts that bureau agents accepted, wages were low, often no more than seven or eight dollars a month for men, plus room and board. Women received even less. Workers were usually paid in a lump sum at the end of the year, both because planters did not have enough cash to pay them every month, and because they wanted to make sure freedmen stayed on the plantation until the crops were harvested. By the time the planter deducted "extra" costs such as medical care or time off for sickness, a worker's pay was often considerably reduced.

Colonel Samuel Thomas, assistant commissioner of the Mississippi Freedmen's Bureau, told Trowbridge that he tried to obtain better wages and conditions for ex-slaves in his district. In the contracts he wrote, Thomas asked that the laborers receive "fifteen dollars a month, with food, including flour, sugar, and molasses; a little patch of ground for each family, and Saturday afternoons [free], for the raising of their own vegetables." Some generous planters agreed to these terms; most did not. (Not all Freedmen's Bureau agents were as fair and conscientious as Samuel Thomas. Some regularly sided with growers in disputes over labor contracts and working conditions.)

In the cotton- and tobacco-growing regions of the South, a form of wage labor called sharecropping became common. Under this arrangement, planters provided freedmen with a piece of land, a place to live, livestock, seed, and farm machinery. In exchange, croppers planted and raised cotton or tobacco, corn, and other grain, and turned the harvest over to the planters. Generally, planters

Many southern planters resisted paying wages to men who had once worked for free as slaves. In this cartoon, a planter demands that a judge—who appears to agree with him—put one of his workers in jail for refusing to work without pay.

would sell the crop and give croppers a quarter to a half of the profit—after deducting expenses. Some planters gave croppers a share of the crop to sell on their own.

Some freedmen became share renters. Unlike sharecroppers, share renters actually owned the crop they planted and sowed. In return for the use of a planter's land, renters had to turn over one-quarter to one-third of their crop to the landowner. But they usually also had to supply their own seed, farm animals, and machinery; the planter provided only land and housing. Because few freed slaves had any money to buy farm animals and supplies, share renting was less common than sharecropping.

Sharecropping may have reduced planters' control over their labor force, but it also freed them from paying cash wages at a time when money was scarce. They could also count on increased productivity from workers who knew that the more abundant the harvest, the more their share would be worth.

Former slaves preferred sharecropping or renting to other forms of wage labor because it allowed them to operate almost independently and freed them from day-to-day supervision by whites. They also hoped that by working hard and saving every penny they could eventually afford to buy or rent land of their own. In all but a few cases, they were disappointed.

The problem was that, even though planters provided them with land and farming supplies, croppers still had to feed and clothe their families. Lacking cash, they had no choice but to buy what they needed on credit from local merchants or planters, promising a portion of their harvest as payment. In a good year, when the weather was fine and cotton prices high, a cropper might be able to give the planter his half of the yield, give the merchants their share to pay off his debts, and still have a little cotton left over to sell.

But the years after the war were not good for sharecroppers. Bad weather led to poor harvests, and by 1868, the prices paid for cotton and other crops had dropped. Cheating by planters also took a large bite out of croppers' income. One candid southern planter explained to Trowbridge how a freedman could be tricked out of his share of the crop. "After the cotton is sent to market, the proprietor calls up his Negroes, and tells them he has furnished them

Articles of Agreement

Entered into this _27th_ day of _March 14_ A. D., 186_6_, between THOMAS J. BROWN & CO., and the undersigned Freedmen, of Giles County, Tennessee, and Limestone County, Alabama, and Philips County, Arkansas.

Witnesseth, That the said THOMAS J. BROWN & CO., have engaged the services of the undersigned, Freedmen, to work on the plantations of said THOMAS J. BROWN & CO., in Giles County, Tennessee, and Limestone County, Alabama, and the plantation of said BROWN, in Philips County, Arkansas, during the year 186_6_, on the following conditions, to wit:

The said THOMAS J. BROWN & CO., hereby agree, jointly and severally, to pay the said Freedmen at the rates and in the manner following, viz:

To each man hired as a 1st class hand, ... $ _15 00_ per month. To each woman hired as a 1st class hand . . . . $ _10 00_ per month.
" " " 2d " " . . . . $ " " " " 2d " " . . . . $
" " " 3d " " . . . . $ " " " " 3d " " . . . . $

One-half the wages to be detained by said BROWN & CO., until the expiration of the year, when the portion so detained shall be paid by the said BROWN & CO., after deducting all indebtedness of the said Freedmen to them.

The said BROWN & CO., hereby agree with said Freedmen, that they will, during the year, maintain, on each of said plantations, a store at which said Freedmen may purchase on credit, to an amount to be fixed by said BROWN & CO., and for cash at all times; and the articles of meat and bread, or meal, shall be sold at said store for cost price.

The said Freedmen hereby agree, severally, that they will work in, and upon said plantations aforesaid, during the year, and obey the orders and instructions of said BROWN & CO., or their authorized superintendents and head-men, and will perform all manner of labor usual in farming and planting, and upon any and every part of said plantations, as they may be from time to time directed by said BROWN & CO., or their authorized agents. That they will continually remain during said year, on said plantation, or either of them, in such buildings as are, or may be provided by said BROWN & CO., and not leave the said plantation during work-hours, without the permission of said BROWN & CO., or their agents, but faithfully work during the day, (which, for the purposes of this contract, begins at sunrise and ends at sunset), with one hours rest at mid-day. And the said Freedmen further agree that they will not ride the work-stock and cattle of said BROWN & CO., without their permission, either at night or on Sunday—and that they shall be charged with all tools lost or wantonly destroyed by them.

The said BROWN & CO., agree to keep superintendents upon each of said plantations who shall, during the year, keep books of the time of said Freedmen, and examine their accounts if they desire it.

And said BROWN & CO., further agree to provide shelter for any such Freedmen as are employed by them, who may be sick and disabled from work, as the fact shall appear on the certificate of a reputable physician; and to provide food, medicine and medical attendance up to the amount that may be due or owing to said sick Freedmen; but said sick Freedmen shall not be entitled to pay during the time they are unable to work.

And the said Freedmen further agree that if they twice absent themselves from work during working hours, the said BROWN & CO., may discharge them without paying them any balance of wages due them; and that at all times the time so lost by any such absence, shall be deducted from the whole working time of the month in which such absence occurs, and the value of it deducted from the pay for that month.

All disputes that may arise between the parties hereto, in reference to matter not provided for in this contract, to be referred for settlement to the Freedmen's Bureau.

In Testimony Whereof, the parties hereto have this day herewith added their hands and seals, on the day and year first above written.

Approved, January 22, 1866.
CLINTON B. FISK, Brevet Maj-Gen., and Ass't. Com. Freedmen's Bureau.

CLASS.	NAMES.	AGE.	Rate of Pay per Month. Dolls. Cents.	CLASS.	NAMES.	AGE.	Rate of Pay per Month. Dolls. Cents.
1st	Amma X Brown	10		1st	James X West	15	
Do	Moses X Anderson	15		Do	Levi X Richards	15	
Do	Sally X Arolala	10		Do	Richard H X Johnson	15	
Do	Chas. X Munday	15		Do	Sarah X West	10	
Do	Sam. X Quisenberry	15		Do	Albat X Thomas	15	
Do	Sealy Ann X Quisenberry	10		Do	Merritt X Drake	15	
Do	Geo. X Davis	15		Do	John X Neely	15	
Do	James X Tilford	15		Do	Dan X Barrett	15	
Do	Geo. X May	15		Do	Margret X Barrett	10	
Do	James X McConnel	15		Do	Beverly X Hill	15	
Do	Benj. X Amos	15		3d	Benj. X Allison	12	
Do	Silas X Harper	15		1st	Robert X Letcher	10	
4	Alfred X Harper	4		Do	Elizabeth X Mead	10	
1st	Mallie X Harper	10		Do	Amanda X Robinson	10	
Do	Andy X Mead	15		Do	Frances X Nelson	10	
Do	Benj. X Hippard	15		Do	James X Williams	15	

The freedmen who signed this labor contract agreed to work for Thomas J. Brown for nine months. Brown held back one-half of each worker's total salary until the end of the year.

such and such things, for which he has charged so much, and that there are no profits to divide."

All too often, remembered Gabe Butler, an ex-slave from Mississippi, "when de end of de year would come, [the croppers] was so deep in debt dey white folks took all dey made."

Planters who cheated their workers used scare tactics to keep them from seeking work on another plantation. "They tell the Negroes that if they go with the agents of the Bureau to other places, the able bodied among them will be carried off and sold into Cuba, and the women and children drowned in the Mississippi," a Georgia bureau agent told Trowbridge.

These tactics rarely worked. Few freedmen would stand for being lied to or cheated. For the first time in their lives, they had a choice—to leave and find work someplace else. One sharecropper who made that choice was George Washington Browning. For the first year after the war, he and his family stayed on at the Browning plantation in Georgia, working for one-sixth of the crop. But when the end of the year came, the family wound up with nothing but debt. They moved to a plantation a mile away, where the planter offered them a slightly larger share of the crop. The Brownings still weren't able to get ahead, so they moved a third time, this time to a plantation whose owner, desperate for good labor, promised them half of the crop. For the first time, the Brownings were able to earn a little above their expenses, and could start saving to buy land of their own.

Most former slaveowners believed freedmen and women could not survive on their own, and that planters were doing them a favor by giving them work and a place to live. They expected their workers to be grateful and to treat them with the same "deference, respect & attachment" they had shown during slavery. Instead, freedmen were bargaining for higher wages and complaining to the Freedmen's Bureau about brutal treatment and unfair labor contracts. That a former slave "should assume to be a man, self-owning and self-directing, was intolerable" to most white Southerners, Trowbridge found.

"The great trouble in this country is, the people are mad at the niggers because they're free," one white Southerner told Trowbridge. "They always believed they wouldn't do well if they were emancipated, and now they maintain, and some of them even hope, they won't do well—that too in the face of actual facts." Trowbridge frequently encountered formerly rich whites who called their former slaves lazy for refusing to work twelve or fifteen hours a day as they had in slavery, and then complained about having to work themselves for the first time in their lives. Freedmen who preferred to work for themselves instead of a white planter were considered slothful.

Far from being lazy, most freedmen who resisted making contracts with planters simply preferred to live as independently as they could. They sought work on railroads, hauling wood, or digging ditches. They trapped, hunted, and fished for game to sell and to feed their families. Even men who worked in the fields often did so only part-time, spending at least a day or two a week working for themselves or enjoying leisure time with their families.

But many planters stubbornly clung to outdated notions about how to manage their workers. M. C. Fulton, a Georgia planter, asked a local Freedmen's Bureau agent to help solve a problem on his plantation: Freedwomen were refusing to work in the fields. These women, Fulton fumed, were "as nearly idle as it is possible for them to be, pretending to spin-knot or something that really amounts to nothing."

Like many planters who made similar complaints, Fulton tried to convince the agent that his true concern was not the size of his labor force, but the welfare of his employees. Black women all worked in the fields during slavery, Fulton pointed out. Rather than allow them to become "idlers" now that they were free, surely "it would be far better for them to go to work for reasonable wages . . . both in regard to health & and in furtherance of their family well-being."

Meanwhile, these "idle women" were raising large families, doing the housework, going to market, cooking the meals, sewing their families' clothes, maintaining the garden that provided their families with fresh vegetables and, if they had any spare time, perhaps taking in laundry for white families to earn extra money. Black women were not necessarily working any less than they had during slavery—they were doing the work *they* chose to do.

Despite friction between employers and employees, bad weather, low crop prices, and crushing debt, the South limped toward recovery. By 1867, cities, homes, barns, bridges, and roads were nearly all rebuilt. Most former slaves were back at work on the plantations under some kind of labor contract. Cotton, tobacco, rice, and other raw materials were once again moving from the South to the North and to Europe.

Even so, it would be years before the region's economy regained its pre-war strength. The harvests of 1865, 1866, and 1867 were far smaller than planters expected—and needed—to rebound from their wartime losses. Nor were northern businessmen investing as

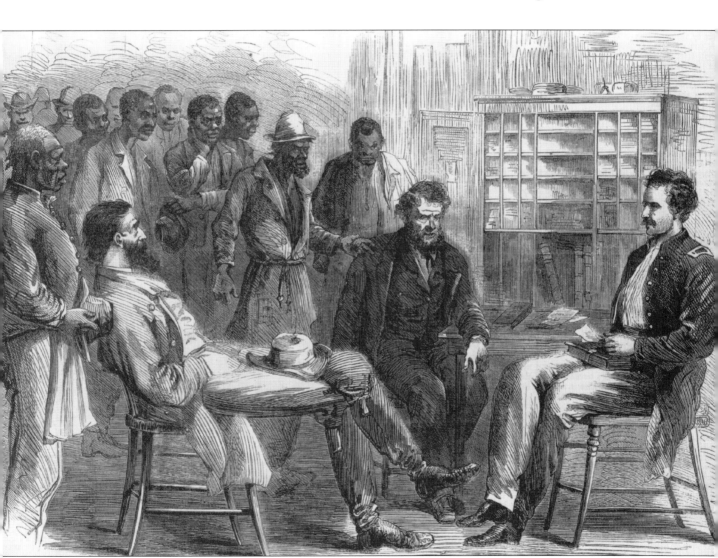

When a disagreement arose between a worker and his employer, both parties often turned to the local Freedmen's Bureau for a decision.

much money in the South as former Confederates had hoped. The high cost of borrowing money, along with labor troubles and uncertain harvests, made doing business in the region too risky.

Two years after the war, neither planters nor freedmen were satisfied with their lot. Planters did not feel as if they had enough

◆ A Losing Venture ◆

Henry Lee Higginson was one of many young, well-educated Northerners who decided to try cotton-raising in the South after the Civil War. Although the former Union Army major hoped to make money, that was not his only motive for moving south. He and his wife also planned to open a school and help educate the newly freed slaves.

Higginson and two army friends agreed to invest in a plantation together. The three men felt sure they could manage a plantation successfully and profitably. They had all had some experience in the South while serving in the army, and Higginson had read several books on the subject of plantation life.

The partners traveled to Georgia in the fall of 1865 and, after a search, found a suitable plantation near Savannah, called Cottonham. Cottonham's owner agreed to sell the five-thousand-acre plantation, which included a fine old house, for thirty thousand dollars.

Higginson and his partners spent the next few weeks hiring additional field hands, buying livestock and other supplies, and painting and furnishing the "big house." Mrs. Higginson joined her husband at the beginning of the new year.

Like other Northerners who moved south right after the war, the Higginsons brought their northern assumptions with them. They assumed that freed slaves would flourish under their firm but kind supervision. They also assumed the freedmen would have no difficulty adapting to the North's free labor system, under which they would work for wages instead of food, clothing, and shelter. The Higginsons' assumptions were soon tested by the reality of working with people whose experiences of life and work had been dramatically different from theirs.

The first sign of trouble arose in February 1866, when it was time to plant the cotton. A number of the field hands at first resisted making labor contracts. "They still do not understand the value of work and wages," Mrs. Higginson wrote in her diary on February 14. "They think they ought to get all their living and wages besides, all extra." Nevertheless, she wrote, she was sure they would come to a clearer way of thinking in time. "They are good, active, honest people, all of them."

control over their work force. And the independence former slaves had hoped freedom would bring still seemed out of reach. Both would look to politics as a way to get what they wanted. The resulting clashes between former masters and former slaves produced the most explosive years of Reconstruction.

Two weeks later, her view was already beginning to change. The black laborers and servants seemed to need constant supervision, she wrote, "and spurring on and urging and [a] system to guide them, which they would not be likely to have of their own accord. However, time will show whether this is merely the result of slavery and dependence, or whether they can ever be wholly independent."

Despite problems with labor and the weather, the cotton crop was planted by April. Mrs. Higginson, meanwhile, had started a school for the children of their employees. Maybe everything would turn out fine, after all.

Less than two weeks into July, however, Henry Higginson realized that the cotton crop would not be as big as he had hoped. August brought constant rain, reducing the crop even further. It was a discouraged man who wrote to his father in December: "We have just about 12,000 lbs. of clean cotton and are done ginning. I find the prices lower and the market very dull here to-day. I am a little puzzled to know what to do. . . . It has cost about $16,500 to make our

Henry Lee Higginson found more problems than profits when he moved south and bought a cotton plantation.

crop, and we shall get $9,000 to $10,000 for it we hope. A good crop at $1.00 a lb. would have given $25,000. There is the whole story."

That spring, Higginson and his partners suffered another blow. It seemed that the man from whom they had bought Cottonham had owned only twenty-five hundred of the five thousand acres he had sold them. Discovering the swindle was the last straw for one of the partners, who left for good. Henry Higginson, too, was ready to pack up and go, but his wife wanted to give life in the South another year. She changed her mind, however, after developing a mild case of malaria, and by July 1867 the Higginsons were on their way north.

Henry Lee Higginson spent the rest of his life in Boston, Massachusetts, working in the safe and predictable profession of banking.

Born a slave, Robert Smalls became a Union war hero and helped write the South Carolina Constitution.

FOUR

• The Power of the Vote •

As he searched for a seat in the Charleston Club House on the morning of January 14, 1868, Robert Smalls must have been struck by the dramatic changes in his life. Only six years before he had been a slave, piloting a Confederate supply ship. Now he was a free man, owner of his own home—and a delegate to the state convention charged with rewriting the South Carolina Constitution.

Looking around after he was settled, Smalls would have observed an extraordinary sight—a room filled with black men and white men whose relation to one another was not that of master and slave. Instead, he and the 123 other delegates had assembled to work toward a common goal—making black and white South Carolinians equal in the eyes of the law.

The delegates represented a remarkable collection of backgrounds and points of view. In addition to Smalls, there were fifty-seven ex-slaves, forty-nine of whom had been born and raised in South Carolina. They included ministers, businessmen, carpenters, blacksmiths, shoemakers, coachmen, barbers, teachers, carriage makers, and waiters. Most could read and write.

Nineteen freeborn black men were also among the delegates. Twenty-six-year-old Robert Brown Elliott, born in Boston, Massachusetts, had attended Eton, an elite school in England. Francis L.

Cardozo, thirty, had been educated at the University of Glasgow in Scotland. A clergyman and teacher sent south by the American Missionary Association, Cardozo was now principal of the largest black school in South Carolina. Another delegate, Richard Harvey Cain, headed the Emanuel African Methodist Episcopal Church of Charleston.

Nearly half of the forty-eight white delegates were native South Carolinians, among them Thomas J. Robertson, a former slaveowner and one of the richest men in the state. Delegate Franklin J. Moses, a member of one of Charleston's wealthiest families, was also there. Moses was said to be the man who pulled down the U.S. flag from over Fort Sumter in April 1861, after Confederate troops defeated the Union force there in the battle that launched the Civil War. By the end of the war, Moses had shifted his support from the Confederacy to the Union, a move that had earned him the hatred of many of his former friends.

Not all the white delegates were wealthy. Some were small farmers like Solomon George Washington Dill from Kershaw. He had supported the Union during the war, and believed that the only way for the poor people of the South to get ahead was for blacks and whites to work together.

Nor were all the white delegates born in the South. A number were northern men who had commanded black troops or worked for the Freedmen's Bureau and decided to settle in South Carolina when the war ended. One such man was Daniel H. Chamberlain, thirty-two, who had attended Harvard and Yale universities and led the Fifth U.S. Colored Cavalry, a black regiment from Massachusetts.

Robert Smalls's background was as impressive as that of any delegate elected to the convention. Born a slave in Beaufort, he had begun working on boats at an early age. By the start of the Civil War, he was serving as a pilot on the *Planter*, a Confederate transport ship that carried ammunition, guns, and other war supplies. In a daring move, Smalls stole the *Planter* while its white captain was attending a party on shore. He piloted the ship out of Charleston harbor and delivered it safely to the Union fleet, which had set up a blockade nearby. Smalls's reward was freedom and a job as pilot on Union warships.

When the war ended, Smalls returned to Beaufort and settled with his young wife, Hannah, and their two daughters, Elizabeth and Sarah, in a house he bought at government auction. The property included the slave quarters where Smalls had been born. The self-taught Smalls hired a private teacher, with whom he studied every day for two hours to complete his education. Much of his time was spent raising money to establish a permanent public school that his daughters and other black children in Beaufort could attend. By 1867, he had enough money to buy and equip a two-story building with eight large rooms, which he deeded to "the colored children of the town."

Smalls got involved in local and national politics even before the end of the Civil War. He was one of sixteen residents of the Sea Islands off the coast of South Carolina who attended the Republican National Convention in Baltimore, Maryland, in June 1864, where he pressed for black suffrage. He was also among the founders of a local Republican Club, the first in South Carolina.

Life seemed good to Smalls and his family the first summer after the war, and they looked toward the future with optimism. Their hope turned to dismay in the fall of 1865 when the newly elected, all-white South Carolina Legislature passed the Black Codes. It was clear to Robert Smalls and other freed slaves that the intent of these laws was to put black men and women back to work on the plantations and under the supervision of white men.

During the fall and winter of 1865–1866, Black Codes of varying severity were enacted in every southern state. The white legislators who passed these laws sincerely believed they were acting in the best interests of both white and black citizens. The fact that slavery had been abolished did not, in the eyes of these lawmakers, mean that former slaves were ready for equality with whites; the changes should be phased in gradually.

Freed slaves had to contend with more than the Black Codes in the first year after the war. Once they had been pardoned, many former rebels lost their fear of the federal government and felt free to express their anger and frustration over losing the war. They unleashed a campaign of harassment and violence against freed slaves and white men who had not supported the Confederacy. Former rebels attacked boldly, knowing that even in the unlikely event that they were arrested and tried, the jury would be composed of sympathetic whites who probably would not convict them.

Black citizens were savagely beaten and killed for the flimsiest of reasons. In Tennessee, a white man named Amos Black told one of his workers, a freedman named Tom, to return to their owner a pair of oxen Black had borrowed. Tom explained that he did not know the way and asked his employer to send Tom's brother, Walker, instead, since he "knew the road."

Black reacted by shooting Tom through the head. Standing over his dead employee, Black said: "You have been fooled with the d——d Yankee lies till you thought you were free, and you got so you would not obey your master. There is no law against killing niggers & I will kill every d——d one I have if they do not obey me and work just as they did before the war."

Freed slaves protested such atrocities to the local Freedmen's Bureau and looked to the federal government for protection. As stories about the Black Codes and the appalling brutality toward freed slaves and white Unionists reached the North, Northerners began to realize that President Johnson had given the former Confederate states too much power too soon. They also realized that the rights of freedmen would never be protected unless the federal government stepped in.

"It seems clear that no northern man, no Yankee can live in the South in any moderate safety yet," observed New Yorker George Templeton Strong. "Negroes are oppressed, tortured, and murdered by their [former] owners. We may have to undertake another civil war."

Radical Republicans in the U.S. Congress were already distressed by President Johnson's leniency toward the former Confederacy. They took advantage of growing public outrage over the Black Codes and anti-Republican violence to challenge Johnson's plan for Reconstruction. Johnson strongly opposed forcing southern states to give freed slaves the right to vote and other civil rights. He felt that, once they renounced slavery and swore loyalty to the Union, these states should be readmitted speedily, without having to meet any more conditions. But the Radicals succeeded in persuading more moderate Republicans, who held a majority in Congress, to support their plan for Reconstruction, which would keep former Confederate states out of the Union until they expanded the rights of former slaves.

Led by powerful anti-slavery crusaders such as Senator Charles Sumner of Massachusetts and Representative Thaddeus Stevens of

VERDICT "HANG THE D— YANKEE AND NIGGER"

Many Southerners blamed Northerners and freedmen for all the South's post-war troubles. This 1867 cartoon graphically expresses their view of how the "d—— Yankee and nigger" should be dealt with.

Pennsylvania, the Radicals pushed a series of laws through Congress in 1866 and 1867 designed to protect and add to the rights of freed slaves, culminating in two "Reconstruction" acts. The Reconstruction laws required southern states to dissolve the all-white governments elected after the war and begin again. This time, they had

◆ Riot in New Orleans ◆

It was just after noon on July 30, 1866, and Republicans—white and black—were holding a convention at the Mechanics' Institute in New Orleans. The delegates were considering amendments to the state constitution that would extend the vote to former slaves—and take it away from former rebels.

Milling around outside the building was a mob of armed and angry white conservatives, including members of the city's police force. The sight of several dozen black marchers coming down the street, carrying a banner that proclaimed them "Friends of the Convention," was all it took for the already edgy conservatives to turn violent. The mob opened fire on the marchers.

The twenty-six delegates and more than one hundred observers inside the institute had no idea what was going on until bullets and bricks began flying through the windows. Suddenly the door was thrown open, and white police burst in and began firing into the crowd.

Just as the police entered,

black merchant L. J. P. Capla, who was inside the building, heard "a [white] woman call out, 'Those dirty Yankees that were sent down here to destroy us, and those niggers—kill them; don't let one of them get away.'" Even though most of the delegates were unarmed, they managed to repel the police several times. But the police kept forcing their way back into the building, shooting and beating more people each time.

Every time the door opened, a few of the people inside managed to run out—only to be shot or kicked or stabbed by a member of the mob waiting outside. No sooner had Edward Campenel, a black woodworker, pushed his way out of the institute than he was grabbed and held by two police officers. "While they were holding me, I was beaten over the head and stabbed. The mob rushed at me crying, 'Kill him, kill him.'"

People inside the building waved white handkerchiefs and begged the police to stop firing. Some pleaded with individual

to write state constitutions that guaranteed the rights of *all* men, black or white, including the right to vote. (Women did not win the right to vote until 1920.)

The southern states had to hold elections in which men of both races were free to register and vote. Once elected, the new state

White conservatives shot down convention supporters in front of the besieged Mechanics' Institute in New Orleans.

policemen to escort them out of the institute to safety. In several cases, policemen agreed, only to shoot or stab or beat the person as soon as they got outside. By the time federal soldiers arrived at 3:00 P.M., thirty-seven black men and three of their white supporters were dead; more than one hundred and fifty people were wounded.

A congressional investigation into the riot revealed that the city's mayor, with support from other local officials and the police, had planned to disrupt the convention. Investigators also discovered that city officials had purposely misled federal military forces stationed nearby about the timing of the convention, so that soldiers arrived too late to stop the killing.

Shock waves from the New Orleans riot reached all the way to Congress, which was still recovering from the news of a bloody race riot in Memphis, Tennessee, four months earlier. The brutality of the two riots helped convince lawmakers that Congress would have to intervene in the South and directly oversee Reconstruction.

lawmakers had to approve the Fourteenth Amendment to the U.S. Constitution, which guaranteed black Americans the same rights of citizenship that white Americans enjoyed.

Then, and only then, would the U.S. Congress readmit the former Confederate states to the Union. To help enforce the Reconstruction laws, Congress stationed federal troops throughout the ten-state region and put Union generals in charge of overseeing these states' political affairs. (The eleventh member of the Confederacy, Tennessee, had been readmitted to the Union in 1866, when its legislature ratified the Fourteenth Amendment.)

Fiercely resentful of congressional attempts to take Reconstruction out of his hands, President Johnson tried to stop the Reconstruction acts from being implemented. Radical members of Congress feared that his interference would prevent their plan from working and tried to have him removed from office. Johnson managed, barely, to hang on to the

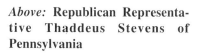

Above: **Republican Representative Thaddeus Stevens of Pennsylvania**

Right: **Along with Thaddeus Stevens, U.S. Senator Charles Sumner, also a Republican, was a powerful supporter of equal treatment for freedmen, and fought tirelessly for a Reconstruction policy that gave freed slaves full rights.**

presidency, but he was no longer powerful enough to block Radical Reconstruction.

Once the Reconstruction laws were passed and federal troops in place, southern states had little choice but to obey them. White conservatives wanted federal troops out of the South, and they wanted their senators and representatives back in Congress so they could have a voice in the national government. They also were hungry for the economic benefits that rejoining the Union could bring. If the only way white Southerners could get what they wanted was by allowing freed slaves to vote, they would no longer stand in the way.

During the fall of 1867, the ten southern states that had not been readmitted to the Union held elections in which black and white citizens could vote for or against holding conventions to rewrite their state constitutions. Those who voted yes could also choose delegates to represent them at the conventions. A majority of voters in all ten states voted to hold conventions.

Robert Smalls helped register voters for the election in Beaufort, South Carolina, where 4,118 of the 4,200 people who turned out for the election voted yes; they also elected Smalls as one of their delegates. Statewide, out of 71,046 South Carolinians who voted—most of them black—68,768 voted in favor of the convention.

Three months after the election in South Carolina, Robert Smalls sat in the Charleston Club House, waiting for the constitutional convention to be called to order. He spent the first week of the convention listening intently to the debate and learning the rules by which political conventions operate. When he felt ready to speak, it was to introduce a motion that would be among the most important of the convention. Rising from his seat in the rear of the hall, Smalls walked down the aisle, turned to face his fellow delegates, and read his proposal. Only four paragraphs long, it called for the state to provide "a system of common schools, of different grades, to be open without charge to all classes of all persons."

Smalls's motion to create South Carolina's first statewide system of free public education was referred to the committee on education, which prepared recommendations and presented them to the entire group for approval. Nearly all the delegates supported Smalls's basic idea, but they passionately disagreed with Smalls and with one another over some of the details.

For one, Smalls proposed that all children between the ages of seven and fourteen be required to attend school for at least six months out of the year. Most white delegates argued that parents should not be forced by the state to do anything they did not want to do—including send their children to school.

Most black delegates, on the other hand, strongly supported making school attendance mandatory. They were convinced that education was vital to their children's eventual success and should not be left up to a parent's whim. "In proportion to the education of the people," declared Alonzo T. Ransier, a shipping clerk and delegate from Charleston, "so is their progress in civilization." Eventually, the delegates agreed to a modified version of Smalls's proposal.

Black delegates were not always on the same side in debates over education and other issues considered during the convention. In the discussion over how to pay for a statewide school system, for example, everyone agreed that property taxes could help cover the cost. Then the committee on education recommended that each male citizen also pay a one-dollar "poll" tax, part of which would be applied to education. Anyone who failed to pay the tax could not vote.

Delegate Robert Brown Elliott rose instantly to protest. "While we may secure the education of our children by adopting the clause as it stands," he said, "we run the risk of depriving many of the parents of the right of suffrage." The state's poorest people, most of whom were black, would not be able to pay the tax, Elliott pointed out. As a result, they would not be able to vote. If the committee insisted on having a poll tax, Elliott said, it should at

Robert Brown Elliott was quick to see the danger in requiring voters to pay a tax before they could cast their ballot.

least add an amendment to protect the voting rights of poor blacks (and poor whites).

Robert C. De Large, another black delegate from Charleston, warned that someday the poll tax might "be used against us for partisan purposes and to our injury." (His prediction was all too accurate. After Reconstruction was over, white officials used the poll tax to prevent black citizens from voting.)

After prolonged debate, the poll tax was passed *with* the amendment suggested by Robert Brown Elliott: "No person shall ever be deprived of the right of suffrage for non-payment of said tax."

Another issue in the debate over education that sparked heated discussion was the proposal that every public school in the state be open to "all the children of the state without regard to race or color." Jonathan J. Wright, a white delegate, argued against including the phrase "without regard to race or color." Creating integrated schools would force "social equality" between blacks and whites too fast, he said, endangering the "peace and harmony" of the state. Prejudice should be allowed to break down naturally, over a period of years, he asserted. Remember, Wright told the group, "We are not framing a Constitution for today, but for years."

Black school principal Francis L. Cardozo vehemently disagreed: "To remove prejudices the most natural method would be to allow children five or six years of age to mingle in school together," he said. "Under such training, prejudice must eventually die out; but if we postpone it until they become men and women, prejudice will be so established that no mortal can obliterate it." The proposal was adopted on the convention's next-to-last day.

On March 14, after fifty-three days of hard work, the constitution was finished. The delegates' final task before going home was to set the date on which South Carolinians could vote for or against the new constitution. On the same day, voters would elect senators and representatives to the state general assembly. They picked April 14, the day Abraham Lincoln was assassinated. April 14 was also the day the Union flag at Fort Sumter was taken down by the Confederates—and the day four years later when it was raised again.

The new South Carolina Constitution was a remarkable document. It awarded the right to vote to all men, regardless of color. This alone put South Carolina far ahead of the North, where, in

1868, twelve of twenty-one states still denied black citizens the right to vote.

The constitution also outlawed Black Codes that limited freed people's choice of work and that permitted physical punishment. And in general, it showed greater concern for people who were poor or disabled than any previous southern (and many northern) state constitutions. No longer could people be sent to prison for failing to pay debts or be denied the right to vote or hold office because they did not own property. State-funded institutions were to be established for those who could not see, speak, or hear. For the first time, a married woman could own property in her own name, instead of her husband's.

Despite the predictions of opponents, the new constitution did not call for the punishment of ex-Confederates or strip them of their right to vote. Speaking before Congress four years after the convention ended, Joseph H. Rainey, the first black man seated in the U.S. House of Representatives, defended the constitution he had helped to write: "Our convention . . . adopted a liberal constitution, securing alike rights to all citizens, white and black, male and female, as far as possible."

Former slaves were jubilant over the outcome of the South Carolina constitutional convention. Former Confederates, on the other hand, reacted with anger, indignation, and fear. Few had taken the convention seriously enough to vote against holding it. During the proceedings, local newspapers had referred dismissively to the gathering as "the great ringed-streaked and striped" convention, the meeting of the "Black and Tan" and the "Great Unwashed," and the "Congo Convention." Delegates were described as "black baboons," "ring-tailed monkeys," and "ragamuffins and jailbirds."

But now that the convention was over and the new constitution a reality, name-calling would not make it go away. Having already lost their wealth, their slaves, their country, and their young men to the war with the Union, former Confederates were now faced with being governed by men they considered "semibarbarians." At best, they believed, black officeholders would be incompetent. At worst, they feared freedmen would perpetrate "dire deeds of riot, rape, robbery, incendiarism and bloodshed" against whites.

The new constitution, moreover, would force white Southerners to pay taxes to send black children to school with their own

> # THE GREAT RING-STREAKED AND STRIPED.
>
> # NEGRO CONVENTION.
>
> ## DESECRATION OF THE CHARLESTON CLUB HOUSE.
>
> Yesterday, according to announcement, the great ringed, streaked and striped convention, called together to provide a new Constitution for the once great State of South Carolina, assembled in, and thereby desecrated, the Charleston Club House, a building erected by a society of Charleston gentlemen, for the enjoyment of each other's company in the pursuit of pleasure.

The Charleston *Mercury* ran daily coverage of the South Carolina constitutional convention under the sneering headline "The Great Ring-Streaked and Striped Negro Convention."

sons and daughters. "The white man may prefer that his children shall be ignorant rather than be debased and corrupted by Negro association," thundered the Charleston *Mercury* at the prospect.

In the days following the close of the convention, conservative white South Carolinians lived in fear of "Negro rule and supremacy at the point of the sword and bayonet." One reported that no man he knew "lives now at his ease. When he lies down at night, although his doors and windows are locked and bolted, he puts his gun and pistol in readiness, not knowing at what hour he may be called upon to use them." Some went so far as to leave the state. "What future can we look forward to for our children?" a resident of Winnsboro, South Carolina, asked. "To live in a land where Free Negroes make the majority of the inhabitants, as they do in this unfortunate state of ours, is to me revolting."

Most former Confederates adopted a more practical approach. Surely they could find some way to keep this ridiculous constitution from being approved by the citizens of South Carolina. On April 2, a group of white South Carolinians held their own convention in the city of Columbia. They condemned the new constitution as "the work of sixty-odd Negroes, many of them ignorant and depraved, together with fifty white men, outcasts of Northern society, and Southern renegades, betrayers of their race and country." They vowed that it would never be ratified.

Conservative whites knew that since South Carolina had more black than white residents, they could not defeat the constitution without support from former slaves. So they set out to convince newly registered freedmen that it was in their best interest to join Democrats in voting against the document. Most whites remained confident that freedmen, who once depended upon slaveowners to meet all their needs, would still listen to their former masters.

"Your present power must surely pass from you," an editorial writer in one Democratic paper warned the freedmen. "It is therefore a most dangerous tool that you are handling. . . . Remember that your race has nothing to gain and everything to lose if you invoke that prejudice which since the world was made has ever driven the weaker tribe to the wall. Forsake then the wicked and stupid men who would involve you in this folly and make yourselves friends and not enemies of the white citizens of South Carolina."

Some white employers threatened to fire any laborer who voted in the election. A mill owner gave his five hired men a week to "decide as to whether or not they would vote." Three of the men being "unwilling to give me a positive answer, I thereupon told them I would dispense with their services." Other planters put language in their labor contracts that forbade laborers to "attend elections or political meetings" without their consent.

Conservatives formed white supremacist organizations such as the Ku Klux Klan, which used violence and intimidation to try to keep freed slaves from voting and exercising other rights. Mounted on horses and disguised by white robes and hoods, Klansmen encircled freedmen's homes, swinging blazing torches and shouting threats. Angry Democrats also broke up Republican political meetings, and beatings and whippings were common.

Southern conservatives did not hesitate to beat, threaten, and even kill black Republicans to keep them away from the polls and out of politics.

"THIS IS A WHITE MAN'S GOVERNMENT."

All these efforts proved futile. Local Republican groups, aided by northern political organizers, had spent countless days mobilizing the black electorate. When election day came, black South Carolinians turned out in overwhelming numbers. Voting was a fundamental expression of their newly won freedom and citizenship; nothing short of murder would keep them from the polls. The evening before the election, towns began to fill up with freed slaves from the surrounding countryside. Before the sun was up the next morning, long lines had already formed outside the polling places.

Nearly all the freedmen who cast ballots voted Republican. They shared the conviction of Robert Smalls, who called the Republican party "the party of Lincoln which unshackled the necks of four millions [of] human beings." They were not swayed by arguments from the men who had fought to keep them enslaved.

When the final votes were counted, the tally was 70,750 for the constitution and 27,288 against; 35,000 registered voters, most of them white, stayed home on election day. The new South Carolina Constitution was now binding.

Planters often fired workers who supported Republican candidates. But freedmen continued to vote for the party that had liberated them and destroyed slavery.

During 1868 and 1869, constitutional conventions also were held in Alabama, Arkansas, Florida, Georgia, Louisiana, Mississippi, North Carolina, Texas, and Virginia. After lengthy and often contentious debates, black and white delegates in each of these states, too, produced new constitutions. Thanks in large part to the high turnout among black voters, all the constitutions were ratified. Although they differed in many respects from the South Carolina document, the constitutions in these states also extended the vote to all men, regardless of color or "previous condition of servitude." In addition, they required free education for all children of school age, and established a wide range of social welfare programs to help their poor and disabled citizens.

At the same time they ratified their new constitutions, southern voters in each state also elected state representatives and senators. Republicans won control of state legislatures and offices throughout the South. In every state, blacks were elected to the legislatures, as well as to other local public offices, such as sheriff, county commissioner, and justice of the peace. Many of these men, including Robert Smalls and Robert Brown Elliott, had served as delegates to the constitutional conventions.

The results of these elections plunged former Confederates into despair. They envisioned state governments overrun by former slaves who would pass laws designed to punish and humiliate white men and to elevate black men. In Alabama, conservatives "set aside the first day the newly elected legislature met for fasting and prayer to Almighty God for the deliverance of the state 'from the horrors of Negro domination.'"

In fact, black Americans never actually controlled a state government during Reconstruction. In South Carolina, one of the few southern states with more black than white residents, blacks held the majority of seats in the house of representatives, but whites controlled the more powerful senate. No black man ever became governor of a reconstructed state and only one was appointed to a state supreme court. Conservative Southerners' dread at the prospect of retribution by vengeful black public officials proved groundless. As Thomas Lee, a former slave and delegate to the Alabama constitutional convention, put it: "I have no desire to take away the rights of the white man. All I want is equal rights in the court house and equal rights when I go vote."

The new state lawmakers handled the first piece of business before them—approval of the Fourteenth Amendment to the U.S. Constitution—with competence and speed. By the middle of the summer of 1868, seven states—Alabama, Arkansas, Florida, Georgia, Louisiana, North Carolina, and South Carolina—had passed the amendment. As promised, the U.S. Congress promptly accepted those states back into the Union. Virginia, Texas, and Mississippi, which had taken longer to pass new state constitutions, did not rejoin the Union until 1869.

Several of the Reconstruction governments stayed in power until 1876. During those years, order was kept, procedures were followed, and laws were passed. Most black legislators, who had begun their careers with little or no experience in debate or lawmaking, learned quickly and carried out their duties effectively.

In many ways, these legislatures helped make the South a more democratic and humane place than it had been before the Civil War. They passed laws to aid poor farmers and laws to guard the rights of black citizens. They created tax policies that charged the rich more and the poor less. They developed generous programs to aid and protect the poor, the disabled, and the disadvantaged. And, in one of their most lasting contributions, Reconstruction legislatures established a network of public schools throughout the South that benefited thousands of children of all races.

The Reconstruction-era legislatures were far from perfect. Some lawmakers, black and white, were corrupt and used their offices to

For the first time, black men could enter politics and directly affect the way their town, county, or state was run. Many, such as the campaigner shown here, found support among former slaves, who now wielded tremendous voting power.

Pictured here are the first black men to serve in the U.S. Congress. After two hundred years of slavery, black Americans finally had a voice in their country's government. Seated from left to right: Senator Hiram R. Revels of Mississippi, Representatives Benjamin S. Turner of Alabama, Josiah T. Walls of Florida, Joseph H. Rainey of South Carolina, and Robert Brown Elliott of South Carolina. Standing: Representatives Robert C. De Large of South Carolina and Jefferson F. Long of Georgia.

gain personal wealth. Others were poorly prepared for the demands of public office. But in general, corruption and incompetence were no more common in Reconstruction governments than in any other state government, then or later.

By 1870, nine years after the Civil War began, the United States was once again united. That year, South Carolina became the first state to send a black representative to Congress—Joseph H. Rainey. Over the next six years, fourteen black congressmen, and two black senators, were elected to Congress from the former Confederacy.

For a short while after the Civil War, the United States came close to living up to the promise contained in the Declaration of Independence—that America would be a country where all men were not only created equal but treated as such. Sadly, this period was not to last.

The intense violence unleashed against southern Republicans convinced many to abandon their homes for the woods or countryside. These black Republicans are living in the relative safety of a Louisiana swamp.

FIVE

◆ *"We Lost All Hopes"* ◆

Gunshots and loud cursing woke South Carolina farmer William Champion out of a sound sleep late one October night in 1870. A man, his face hidden by a mask, shook him roughly and said, "Get up, we have come after you, you damned old radical." It was a few days before the November elections, and Champion was a Republican and an election officer.

As many as fifty masked men stormed through his house, shooting their pistols and destroying everything they could break, smash, or rip apart.

One of the men told Champion to get dressed, and afterward dragged him outside. The group forced him to walk with them for two miles. Finally, they reached a clearing by a river, where they stopped and blindfolded him. One of the men told the terrified farmer he had only minutes to live. They tore off his shirt and pants and whipped him across the back and legs until he nearly passed out. They struck him on the head with their pistols and choked him violently.

Champion survived the beating, but remained so afraid of another attack that for the next nine months he slept in the woods. Most of his Republican neighbors, white and black, were doing the same.

After Reconstruction governments were elected in all the former

Confederate states in the late 1860s, white Democrats used terror and violence to try to regain control. Former slaves who had voted the Radical ticket were warned not to make the same mistake again. Thousands of white Republican voters received visits like the one paid to William Champion.

Samuel White of Spartansburg, South Carolina, was one. The men who beat White demanded that he "alter his principles to a Democrat" and announce his change of heart in the local Democratic newspaper. If he did not, his attackers cautioned the fifty-four-year-old carpenter, they would visit him again. Fearing another whipping or even death, White placed the following notice in the *Spartan*:

> *Mr. Editor:*
>
> *I desire to make this public announcement of my withdrawal from all affiliation with the Republican Party, with which I have heretofore acted. . . . I am prompted to take this step from the conviction that the policy of said party, in encouraging fraud, bribery, and excessive taxation, is calculated to ruin the country.*
>
>

Respectfully,
SAMUEL F. WHITE

In the months following the 1870 election, forty-five Republican residents of Spartansburg published similar announcements.

The "night riders" who terrorized William Champion and Samuel White went by different names in different states: the Ku Klux Klan in Tennessee, Georgia, and the Carolinas; the Knights of the White Camellia in Louisiana; the Knights of the Rising Sun in Texas; and the White Line in Mississippi. Between 1868 and 1871, members of these groups bullied, whipped, beat, shot, stabbed, and murdered thousands of black and white Republicans across the South.

The men who joined the Klan and groups like it were mostly former rebel soldiers who could not stomach the prospect of rule by what they considered to be a collection of know-nothing ex-slaves, greedy Northerners, and southern "traitors." The men who led the Klan were often prosperous, well-educated landowners and professionals.

General John B. Gordon, reputed to be the Grand Dragon of

the Georgia Ku Klux Klan, was a former commander in the Confederate Army and one-time candidate for governor of Georgia. He blamed the explosion of anti-black and anti-Republican violence on "carpetbaggers." Carpetbaggers, according to Gordon and other conservatives, were Northerners who stuffed their few belongings into a cheap suitcase made of carpet and moved south after the Civil War, hoping to make a quick profit at the expense of defeated Confederates. Even worse, conservatives believed, the Northerners incited freed slaves with talk of politics and voting.

"We never had any apprehension from the conduct of the Negroes until unscrupulous men came among them and tried to stir up strife," Gordon maintained. "We can get along with the Negro, loving him, and having him love us, if you will just take away these 'carpetbaggers'."

But as long as Northerners continued to "incite" former slaves, Gordon argued, southern whites needed a "brotherhood—a combination of the best men of the country, to act purely in self defense, to repel the attack in case we [and our families] should be attacked by these people."

Twenty-year-old Henry Henderson, a white man from Columbia, South Carolina, received a more accurate description of this "brotherhood" from men pressuring him to join the KKK. "They were for a white man's government," Henderson recalled. They believed "there was but one way to get it, and that was to kill out and beat out all the colored people and all the white Republicans that voted the Republican ticket." Although threatened with death, Henderson refused to become a Klansman.

The Klan did not confine its attacks to men who made the mistake of voting Republican. Freedmen who had achieved any kind of success or standing in the community, who had become teachers, ministers, or landowners, for example, or who stood up for their rights, were also frequent targets of Klan violence.

A Georgia blacksmith named Dannon was beaten for the crime of being "insolent" to a white man. Dannon had been shoeing horses for a white man named Kemp for an entire year, but had not been paid one cent. One day he told Kemp that he would do no more work until he was paid. A few nights after Dannon made his announcement, he received a "visit" from a group of "disguised men."

In Noxubee County, Mississippi, on a September night in 1868, seven Klansmen broke into the home of Jerry Brown. Brown was a black preacher with "considerable influence among his people." As he lay in bed next to his wife, four of the men shot Brown at close range. A fifth refrained from firing because, he said, the preacher was by then "too dead to shoot at."

In the same county two years later, Klansmen burst into the cabins of five freedmen, beating four severely and killing the fifth.

◆ Memoirs of a Klansman ◆

When the Ku Klux Klan summoned William Lumpkin of Greene County, Georgia, he answered the call promptly. A Confederate veteran who remained intensely loyal to the "Cause," Lumpkin was proud to be asked to join the secret brotherhood of white supremacists.

At his initiation, Lumpkin had to swear his absolute commitment to a white man's government, and promise never to reveal his membership in the Klan or any of the group's "signs, grips, passwords, mysteries, or purposes."

Years later Lumpkin told his daughter, Katharine Du Pre Lumpkin, that no matter what his personal obligations, on "nights when a call came to him, he would mount his horse and ride toward a deep forest or some remote abandoned building, on the way donning his mask and covering his horse so that he

Members of the Klan and other white supremacist groups often disguised themselves with white hoods and robes.

"All of the victims of these outrages were renters of land," reported a local Republican, "and while these Democrats were beating them they constantly reminded them . . . that they had no right to rent land like white folks." Some black landowners were so frightened by these visits that they sold their land or moved to the city and let the land lie unplanted.

Also subjected to Klan outrages were northern white teachers and missionaries who had come south to teach freedmen. In

might arrive white-robed and white-hooded." The robes served as disguises, and Klansmen also hoped the costumes would convince freed slaves that the riders were not men but ghosts.

Once the silent company had assembled, Lumpkin recalled for Katharine and his other children, the horsemen would set out on their midnight mission. "They would ride up to a remote cabin in their horrendous white robes, looking like enormous hobgoblins. . . . They would call a man out of his cabin—a Negro who had voted Republican and talked boastfully about it . . . or one who had been insufferably impudent to a white man." If necessary, some of the robed men would dismount and drag their victim out by force.

Once the man was outside, Lumpkin said, he and the other Klansmen "would begin to talk among themselves so that the man could hear them. One figure would speak of how he had died at Gettysburg or some other

battle and how thirsty he got in hell. Then he would order the quivering man to bring water, buckets of water. One of the robed horsemen would take the bucket of water and drink and drink; then he would ask for another and drink it. Gallon after gallon the trembling man would bring; gallon after gallon to all appearances would go down the gullet of the great white figure, though in truth it . . . trickled out along the shadowy ground through a convenient little hose which the rider had brought along."

Before the night riders left, they would "tell the Negro what was expected of him in 'good behavior'." If the visit was successful, Lumpkin told his children, the man would give white Southerners "no more trouble." He would either move away, or "return to his former humility."

If not, he would be paid another visit—and this time dealt with more harshly.

I AM
COMMITTEE

1st. No man shall squat negroes on his place unless they are all under his employ male and female.

2d. Negro women shall be employed by white persons

3d. All children shall be hired out for something.

4th. Negroes found in cabins to themselves shall suffer the penalty.

5th. Negroes shall not be allowed to hire negroes.

6th. Idle men, women or children, shall suffer the penalty.

7th. All white men found with negroes in secret places shall be dealt with and those that hire negroes must pay promptly and act with good faith to the negro. I will make the negro do his part, and the white must too.

8th. For the first offence is one hundred lashes—the second is looking up a sap lin.

9th. This I do for the benefit of all young or old, high and tall, black and white. Any one that may not like these rules can try their luck, and see whether or not I will be found doing my duty.

10th. Negroes found stealing from any one or taking from their employers to other negroes, death is the first penalty.

11th. Running about late of nights shall be strictly dealt with.

12th. White man and negro, I am everywhere. I have friends in every place, do your duty and I will have but little to do.

Klansmen distributed menacing flyers, such as the one above, to frighten and intimidate black and white citizens alike.

Greensboro, Georgia, the Klan threatened to kill a schoolteacher named Gladden unless he left town. Besides educating freed slaves, Gladden had enraged the local citizenry by walking down the main street holding his umbrella over a black woman.

Republican officials organized state militias and posses to try to stop the Klan. But with the exception of Tennessee and Arkansas, where strong-willed governors succeeded in quelling the worst of the violence, officials were unable to control the night riders.

Sometimes, this was because the law officers themselves were

Ku Klux Klansmen are about to shatter this peaceful scene in a black family's home. During the early years of Reconstruction, the Klan used such nighttime "visits" and other terrorist tactics—including murder—to intimidate black citizens.

night riders, or respected the men who were. In other cases, local officials were simply afraid to challenge the Klan. A sheriff from Fayette County, Alabama, reported that each time he and his men returned from looking for Klansmen, his wife would greet him at the door "crying, saying that they have been there shooting into the

These Ku Klux Klansmen, wearing their nightmarish disguises, have taken their victim deep into the woods.

house. When we scatter to our houses," the sheriff said, "we do not know at what time we are to be shot down; and living with our lives in our hands this way, we have become disheartened, and do not know what to do."

Even when state lawmen were brave enough to arrest night riders, the fear of retaliation made it impossible to find witnesses who would testify against them, or juries that would convict them. Typically, any Klansman who was brought to trial would arrive in court accompanied by "forty or fifty men to swear that he was at some other place" on the night the attack occurred.

Desperate southern Republicans turned to the federal government for help in restoring law and order. Congress responded by passing two enforcement laws that gave the president, the army, and the federal courts the legal authority to put the Klan out of business. Across the South in 1871 and 1872, federal authorities arrested thousands of Klansmen. Some six hundred major offenders were tried, although most got light sentences. By 1872, the Ku Klux Klan and organizations like it were largely out of action—for the time being.

The steps the federal government took to stop the Klan seemed to show that Congress and the White House were still solidly behind the Reconstruction governments and efforts by freed slaves to achieve equality. But this was misleading. Except for a handful of Congressmen like Thaddeus Stevens (who died in 1868) and Charles Sumner, the government's commitment to full civil and political rights for black Americans was minimal. White Northerners' support for Radical Reconstruction was based more on a desire to punish white Southerners for their disloyalty than to give equality to former slaves. As memories of the Civil War faded, the administration and most Republicans in Congress gradually lost interest in the South and the never-ending "Negro question."

By 1873, most Northerners were absorbed by troubles closer to home: A combination of inflation, high taxes, and bad debts had halted the stunning economic growth the North had enjoyed during and since the Civil War. Suddenly, solving problems of massive unemployment, growing labor unrest, and falling crop prices seemed far more important than making sure ex-slaves were able to vote.

The truth, one Republican politician said a year later, "is that our people are tired out with this worn out cry of 'Southern outrages'!!!

Hard times & heavy taxes make them wish the 'nigger,' 'everlasting nigger,' were in ____ or Africa."

White Republicans in the South were also becoming disenchanted with Reconstruction governments. The high cost of the social programs they had created—and the heavy taxes needed to pay for those programs—drove more and more poor and middle-income white Republicans into the Democratic camp.

The southern Republican party—an unlikely mix of transplanted Northerners, freed slaves, and southern Unionists—was weakened further by fighting among its own members over which policies to pursue, how to run state governments, and who would get the best jobs. Party members routinely denounced each other in public, stormed out of meetings, and got into fistfights. Such behavior did little to advance party unity.

While southern Republicans bickered, the Democratic party grew stronger and stronger. Its members had a common goal: to bring down the hated Radical governments. Republican weakness and Democratic unity, combined with ongoing violence and intimidation by white conservatives during election campaigns, help explain how the Democrats managed to win back control of one southern state after another during the 1870s. North Carolina, Tennessee, and Virginia elected Democratic state governments in 1870; Texas in 1873; and Alabama and Arkansas in 1874.

The success of the Democrats in the 1875 Mississippi elections was the beginning of the end for Radical Reconstruction. Mississippi Democrats planned the campaign carefully. They knew that, since more blacks than whites lived in their state, they would have to mount a no-holds-barred effort to wrest control from the Republicans. The Democratic campaign slogan was "Carry the election peaceably if we can, forcibly if we must." Their goal was to frighten white, and especially black, Republicans into voting Democratic or staying away from the polls altogether.

Powerful members of state Democratic organizations, some of them former Confederate generals, organized young men into military-like Democratic "clubs." They equipped them with high-powered rifles and cannon and drilled them in public places, hoping to intimidate Republican voters. For months before the November election, members of these clubs roamed through heavily Republican

Here, white Democrats use guns to "help" a black voter decide how to cast his ballot.

counties, disrupting political meetings, "menacing voters and discharging their guns by night as well as by day."

More than once, these disruptions blew up into full-scale riots. One of the bloodiest occurred in the town of Clinton on September 4, at a Republican-sponsored barbecue featuring speeches by candidates from both parties. The barbecue drew a large crowd, as many as twenty-five hundred people, including women and children. The majority were black Republicans, but many whites had come as well.

Eugene B. Welborne, a black farmer and state representative who attended the barbecue, remembered that the audience listened politely to the first speaker, a Democrat. But the next candidate, a white Republican named H. T. Fisher, had barely begun to speak when two young white men began heckling him. "Come down out of there, you God damned radical, you. We don't want to hear any more of your lies," they yelled. Welborne recognized the men as Democrats from the neighboring town of Raymond, and assumed they had been sent to stir up trouble.

The hecklers, one of whom took periodic swigs from a bottle of whiskey, continued to interrupt the speaker. A black deputy, one of thirty men appointed to keep peace at the meeting, warned the two that he would arrest them if they did not keep quiet. As the deputy spoke, a group of twenty or thirty more white men from Raymond formed a line on either side of the two troublemakers, who continued to harass the speaker. When the deputy tried to make good his threat and arrest the hecklers, one of the men in the line drew a gun and shot him. "As soon as the deputy fell," remembered Welborne, "every man in the line pulled out their pistols and began to fire on the crowd."

For the next two days, said Welborne, the Democratic clubs "just hunted the whole county clean out." Estimates as to the number of black Republicans killed during the riot ranged from thirty to fifty.

With similar atrocities occurring in counties throughout Mississippi, terrified and angry Republicans demanded protection from Governor Adlebert Ames, a Republican from Maine who had won the Congressional Medal of Honor during the war.

Convinced that only federal intervention could halt the violence, Ames wrote to President Ulysses S. Grant and asked him to send troops. The president expressed sympathy, but turned down his request. "The whole public are tired out with these annual autumnal outbreaks in the South," the U.S. attorney general wrote to Ames on the president's behalf. "The great majority are now ready to condemn any interference on the part of the government. . . . Preserve the peace by the forces in your own state."

Left with no alternative, Ames formed and armed several companies of state militia. The first company was led by Charles Caldwell, a blacksmith and ex-slave who had been a delegate to the Mississippi constitutional convention and a member of the state senate since 1869. The reaction from Democrats was immediate.

"The Democrat party has been like roaring lions" since the militia was formed, one black militia member from Vicksburg wrote the governor. "They have sworn to not let us colored militia organize into this city and have been going with their guns . . . round the halls to see if any of them are gathered together, to break them up, and making their threats."

The fear of even greater bloodshed prompted Governor Ames to make a "peace agreement" with the Democrats. The Republican militia companies would disband and give up their arms as long as the Democrats agreed not to interfere with the upcoming elections. Few citizens, Republican or Democrat, took the agreement seriously or believed it would stop the violence. Indeed, the threats and assaults against Republican candidates and voters increased as election day approached.

One day a few weeks before the election, George Glenn, a black candidate for justice of the peace in Madison County, Mississippi, was approached by a white man who offered to pay him to withdraw from the race. "No, sir, not for ten thousand dollars," replied Glenn. "As the people have placed confidence in me I am going to run until I am beat." The white man told Glenn he would "be beat anyhow, because if you get it you are a dead man and if you don't get it you are a dead man." Glenn replied that he would run no matter what the risk. The man left him with a threat: "A rope will pull your neck after this campaign."

Late that night, a friend woke Glenn from a sound sleep to warn him that a group of whites was after him. "I ran out in my drawers and undershirt," said Glenn, "into a cotton patch about a mile from the house. They came and fired—we could see them—they fired and fired into the house. As they were going off I heard them say, 'We haven't got him now, but we will get him.'" George Glenn survived the election, although he lost to a Democrat.

The night before the election, armed riders rampaged through Mississippi's Republican counties, warning black citizens that they would be killed if they showed up to vote. Robert Gleed, a former state senator who was running for sheriff of Lowndes County, remembered that in his city "three buildings were set on fire and four men killed. Most of the colored people were run out of their houses during the night. . . . It was the most violent time that ever we have seen."

When election day dawned on November 2, large numbers of white men brought their guns to the polls, ready to drive black voters away. At several polling booths, conservatives had cannon in place.

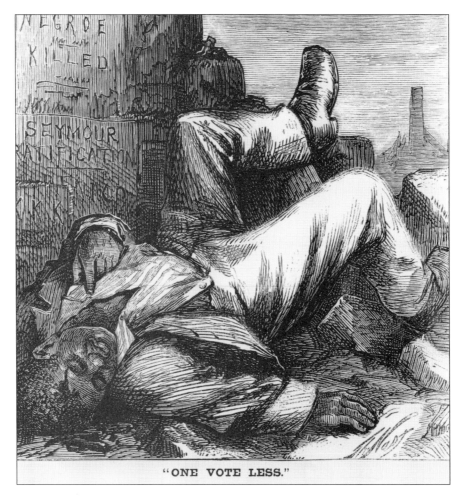

"ONE VOTE LESS."

Published in a southern newspaper, this drawing illustrated the violence that marred southern elections during Reconstruction.

"We could hear in the morning the cannons commencing to shoot in every direction," recalled Eugene Welborne. "You could see men with their sixteen-shooters buckled on them charging all through the country." All day long, said Welborne, squads of these men came in from other counties with horror stories designed to frighten black Republicans into voting Democratic or not voting at all. "One hundred and fifty niggers killed in Raymond; one white man slightly wounded," one report said. The word from Jackson was that "the white men have whipped the niggers and run them out."

Black voters had no way of knowing that these accounts were either lies or highly exaggerated, and they were frightened. At one point, a dispirited Welborne approached black state Senator Charles Caldwell, who was observing the voting in the town of Clinton. He suggested to the senator that, in the interest of safety, perhaps Republican election officials should tell everyone to go home. "No. We are going to stay right here," Welborne remembered Caldwell telling him.

Caldwell's courage inspired other black voters, who cast their ballots despite the threats. "We would have polled our usual vote, even with all the intimidation, if they would have let us," said Welborne. But the Democrats managed to drive off the Republican registrars by telling them that "it would not be healthy for them to serve." They replaced them with Democrats who, each time a Republican voter came forward, told him that his name was not in the book of registered voters and turned him away.

W. H. Bell, a black lawyer and Republican election registrar in Hinds County, remembered seeing a black Republican he knew wearing a Democratic badge. "What does this mean?" Bell asked his friend.

"I am as good a Republican as you are," the frightened man replied, "but I am obliged to vote this ticket."

Even in Mississippi counties where large numbers of men found the courage to cast their ballots for Republican candidates, Democrats frequently found ways to influence the results in their favor. At 11:00 P.M., after the polls had closed in Hinds County, Bell and the other registrars (all white) were counting the votes when a heavily armed white man drinking whiskey entered the courthouse.

"Well, now, I must confess, though not a coward," said Bell, "that I felt some intimidation, so much so that I left the board of registration in charge of the Democratic registrar and never returned." Once Bell was gone, the Democrats were free to remove or destroy Republican ballots and replace them with their own.

In other efforts to ensure Democratic majorities, men voted as many as four times, using different names; men under twenty-one, the legal voting age at the time, lied about their age and cast ballots for Democrats.

The outcome of the Mississippi state elections of 1875 surprised no one. Democrats carried county after county where Republicans had held majorities only two years before. In 1873, 1,300 Republicans

Federal voting officials and a soldier watch closely as votes are counted in a southern election. Their presence was necessary to keep Democrats from adding extra votes or destroying Republican ballots.

had voted in Coahoma County; in 1875, only 230 cast ballots. In Hinds County, the number of Republican voters fell that year by 1,100. In Yazoo County, it dropped from 2,500 to 7.

The violence did not end with election day. Despite the brutal effectiveness of the "Mississippi Plan," one Republican had been reelected to the U.S. Congress and almost a third of the state's counties were still controlled by Republicans. As they tried to carry out their duties, many of the new Republican officeholders were confronted by Democratic vigilantes who told them to resign or be killed. Some Republicans and their families, including W. H. Bell, were driven from the state. Others, like Charles Caldwell, who refused to leave his state or his position as state senator, were murdered.

By the time Mississippi returned to Democratic hands in 1875, Reconstruction governments remained in only three southern states—South Carolina, Louisiana, and Florida. Democrats there were emboldened by the success of the Mississippi Plan—and by the federal government's unwillingness to intervene and ensure fair elections. During the next state elections in 1876, conservatives in all three states resorted openly to economic intimidation, violence, riots, and fraud to unseat Republicans.

Despite the danger, in all three states enough Republicans braved the polls on election day to produce results so close that both Democrats and Republicans claimed victory. In South Carolina and Louisiana, both parties set up a legislature and installed a governor—and sent petitions to Washington demanding that they be recognized as the official winner.

South Carolina, Louisiana, and Florida were also at the center of the controversy surrounding the 1876 U.S. presidential race between Democrat Samuel Tilden and Republican Rutherford B. Hayes. As in the state elections, both sides claimed that their candidate had won. Hayes needed to carry all three states to win the election; Tilden needed just one.

Democrats insisted that Tilden should be declared president, since he had won the majority of votes in each of the three states. "One hundred thousand armed men would march to Washington to see that Mr. Tilden was inaugurated," declared Representative Henry Watterson of Kentucky in a speech to Congress. "Tilden or War" became the rallying cry in many Democratic newspapers.

Republicans countered that the only reason Tilden wound up with

Charges of widespread voting fraud in the South left the 1876 U.S. presidential election up in the air. Republican Rutherford B. Hayes, pictured here, was finally declared the winner.

Under orders from President Hayes, federal troops leave New Orleans. With the departure of troops from the South, no one was left to protect and enforce Reconstruction reforms.

more votes was because the Democrats had used intimidation, violence, and fraud to get them.

Fevered negotiations between the two sides produced no results, and by late January 1877 the country still had no president-elect. Citizens were bewildered and not a little panicked. Who was running the country? Would there be another civil war? Freedmen and women were especially alarmed; many believed that if the Democrats won the presidency slavery would be reestablished.

Finally, Congress had to step in. It created a commission to review the disputed presidential election returns in each of the three states and decide whether the states should go to Tilden or Hayes. Five senators, five representatives, and five Supreme Court justices were appointed to the commission, which found substantial evidence of Democratic fraud. Commission members voted eight to seven that all three southern states should be credited to the Republicans.

Democrats refused to accept the decision, still convinced that they had been robbed of the presidential election. Just when it began to look as if the standoff would go on forever, representatives of both parties, negotiating behind the scenes, reached an agreement that if adopted would put Hayes in the White House. This "plan of peace" assured the South of federal aid to finish its railroad system, as well as other building projects, and prominent positions for Democrats in the federal government. Most important, from the

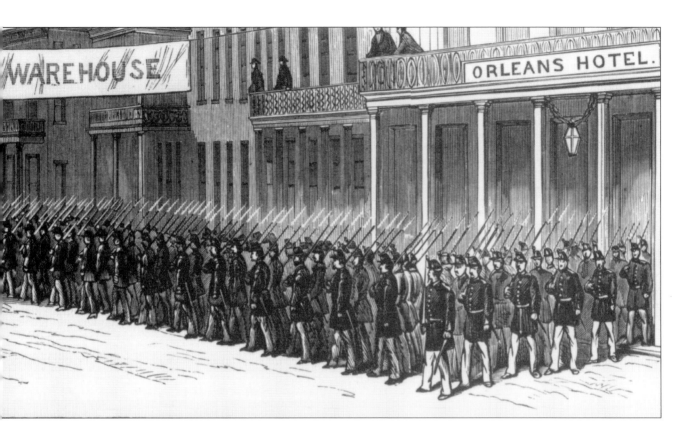

Democrats' point of view, the agreement would return "home rule" to the South. The few federal troops remaining in the cities of South Carolina and Louisiana would be ordered back to their barracks, leaving Democrats fully in charge. No troops were stationed in Florida at the time.

In return, the Democratic governors elected in South Carolina and Louisiana pledged to protect the rights of black citizens.

Both parties accepted the Compromise of 1877, as the agreement was called, and Rutherford B. Hayes became president of the United States on March 4, 1877. As promised, one of his first acts was to order federal troops out of southern cities. With the troops gone, Democrats in Louisiana and South Carolina triumphantly reclaimed the statehouses in their respective capitals. Reconstruction was over.

It was a terrible moment for freedmen and women. "In 1877, we lost all hopes," said Henry Adams, a former slave from Alabama. "The whole South—every state in the South—had got into the hands of the very men that held us slaves."

By 1877, the year Reconstruction ended, the South was once again producing goods for trade with the North and Europe. These bales of cotton are being loaded onto a ship in Charleston, South Carolina.

SIX

• *The Legacy of Reconstruction* •

*B*y the end of the nineteenth century, few signs remained of
the great conflict that had taken place in the South more than
thirty years earlier. Businesses, homes, churches, farms, bridges,
and railroads destroyed during the Civil War had been rebuilt.
Cotton, tobacco, sugar cane, and rice flourished in once-bare fields.
Textile mills, coal mines, and sawmills were helping the South's
economy expand beyond agriculture. The few physical reminders
of the war—the abandoned trenches and earthworks scattered over
the landscape—had become playgrounds for children to whom the
Civil War was just a story their grandparents told.

Slavery was a thing of the past, and the eleven states of the former
Confederacy had been reinstated as full members of the United States.
Once again, goods, services, ideas, information, and people flowed
between the two regions. Aging Confederate and Union veterans
swapped war stories instead of gunfire.

Most important, white Southerners once again thought of themselves as Americans. For them, the reunification of the North and
South had become an emotional as well as a legal reality.

Few of the four million freed slaves whose fate had been at
the heart of the Civil War benefited from this renewed spirit of
unity. As one former slave woman put it, if black Americans had

"started up the hill" during Reconstruction, with its end they "went right back down again."

Some progress had been made. The number of black landowners, businessmen, and professionals had increased, and more black Southerners than ever before knew how to read and write. But the great majority of former slaves still lived in poverty, barely able to keep themselves and their families fed, clothed, and sheltered. Most black men could not get work except as field hands or unskilled laborers; women's choices were generally limited to housekeeping, cleaning, or cooking for white families. Those who sought better paying jobs in industries such as textiles were generally turned away or offered only the lowest paying and least skilled work.

The Freedmen's Bureau had been disbanded in 1872. With bureau agents and federal troops no longer on the scene to protect freed slaves, white planters felt free to write restrictive labor contracts, use physical punishment, and create slave-like working conditions.

Another source of labor for planters and other large employers was the convict leasing program. This system allowed employers to "lease" prisoners from the state. The convicts, who spent their sentences working instead of serving time in prison, were mostly black men who had been arrested for petty crimes. They generally worked in "chain gangs," in which each man was chained to the next.

State officials liked convict leasing because it saved them the cost of housing and feeding prisoners. Employers liked the system because it provided them with a cheap, easily controlled labor force. The men who labored in chain gangs were worked literally to death—the mortality rate among southern prisoners "leased" to planters and other employers was nine times the rate in northern prisons. "This place is nine kinds of hell," one convict wrote of his life in the lease system.

The years after Reconstruction also saw a steady erosion of freedmen's voting rights. Now that they were back in charge, white Southerners had no intention of letting black citizens threaten their hold on power again. They also continued to believe, despite the evidence of the Reconstruction governments, that black men were not fit to vote or hold office.

To most southern whites, black suffrage was a threat to peaceful, civilized society in the South. "When men's property, their peace

A chain gang cleans the streets of Richmond, Virginia, in preparation for the arrival of President Hayes.

and all that they hold dear, are endangered," wrote Democrat Edward Ward Carmack, editor of the influential Nashville *American* newspaper, "they will defend them, no matter in what form the aggression may come—whether as a highwayman with a bludgeon or a Negro with a ballot."

Many white conservatives favored enacting laws to take the vote away from black men. What was needed, argued Mississippi State Senator James Z. George, were measures that would "invest permanently the powers of government in the hands of the people who ought to have them—the white people." But there was a major roadblock to this plan: the Fifteenth Amendment to the Constitution, adopted in 1870, which guaranteed all men the right to vote, regardless of race.

The federal Constitution was the law of the land, overriding all state laws. Any southern state that defied the Constitution by passing a law explicitly denying black citizens the vote was inviting federal intervention. Even a federal government that had washed its hands of the "Negro problem" probably would not ignore such blatant disregard of the Constitution. The challenge for white Southerners, then, was to figure out a way to disqualify blacks from voting that was not obviously based on race.

The most common strategies adopted by southern legislators

◆ Exodus ◆

John Solomon Lewis and his family were among thousands of former slaves who left Louisiana, Mississippi, Texas, and Tennessee in the spring of 1879 to seek "real" freedom in Kansas. These "Exodusters," as they were called, were escaping poverty, debt, and the brutal racial discrimination and violence of the post-Civil War South.

Since the war, Lewis had farmed a piece of land he rented from a white man in Tensas Parish, Louisiana. When the harvest was sold, the Lewis family was supposed to get a share of the proceeds. But no matter how hard the family worked or how large a crop they produced, they ended each year deeper in debt to the planter.

One day, Lewis worked up his courage and told the landowner he was leaving. "I works hard and raises big crops," he said, "and you sells it and keeps the money, and brings me more and more debt, so I will go somewhere else and try to make headway like white workingmen."

The angry landowner warned

Lewis that if he tried to leave "you will get your head shot away." That night, Lewis, his wife, and their four children took "to the woods" along the banks of the Mississippi River. They stationed themselves near a wharf, and settled down to wait for a boat that would take them to St. Louis, Missouri, where they could catch the train for Kansas. Lewis had heard there was free land to homestead in Kansas, and that it was a place where a poor man, black or white, could get a decent start.

During their three-week wait, the Lewises were joined by dozens of other black families also hoping to make their way to Kansas. But no boats would stop for them. Southern planters, furious over losing their labor force, had convinced Mississippi riverboats not to pick up the Exodusters.

Most of the families had brought little food or extra clothing with them. As they waited for weeks, sometimes months, for a boat to stop, many came close to starvation.

One day, a boat did pull up near where the Lewises were camped. But as the family boarded, the

were poll taxes and literacy tests. Starting with the elections in 1892, for example, every Mississippian who went to the polls had to pay a two-dollar tax before casting his ballot. Since few black residents had two dollars to spare, the poll tax prevented many from voting—just as Robert C. De Large had predicted it would back at the

captain tried to turn them back. Lewis stood his ground, saying, "I am a man who was a United States soldier and I know my rights, and if I and my family gets put off, I will go in the United States Court and sue for damages.

"Says the captain to another boat officer, 'Better take that nigger or he will make trouble.'"

The crew allowed the Lewises to board and begin their journey to Kansas.

Life in Kansas was not perfect, but by 1900 the Exodusters were better off economically, socially, and politically than freed slaves who had stayed in the South. They earned higher wages, and many were able to buy their own homes. And, although they still faced racial discrimination, it was nothing like the cruel treatment they had endured in the South.

The migration of freed slaves from the South did not end with the Kansas Exodus of 1879. Between 1880 and 1910, more than five hundred thousand left the region, heading north and west in search of a better life.

All Colored People

THAT WANT TO

GO TO KANSAS,

On September 5th, 1877,

Can do so for $5.00

IMMIGRATION.

WHEREAS, We, the colored people of Lexington, Ky,. knowing that there is an abundance of choice lands now belonging to the Government, have assembled ourselves together for the purpose of locating on said lands. Therefore,

BE IT RESOLVED, That we do now organize ourselves into a Colony, as follows:— Any person wishing to become a member of this Colony can do so by paying the sum of one dollar ($1.00), and this money is to be paid by the first of September, 1877, in instalments of twenty-five cents at a time, or otherwise as may be desired.

RESOLVED, That this Colony has agreed to consolidate itself with the Nicodemus Towns, Solomon Valley, Graham County, Kansas, and can only do so by entering the vacant lands now in their midst, which costs $5.00.

RESOLVED, That this Colony shall consist of seven officers—President, Vice-President, Secretary, Treasurer, and three Trustees. President—M. M. Bell; Vice-President —Isaac Talbott; Secretary—W. J. Niles; Treasurer—Daniel Clarke; Trustees—Jerry Lee, William Jones, and Abner Webster.

RESOLVED, That this Colony shall have from one to two hundred militia, more or less, as the case may require, to keep peace and order, and any member failing to pay in his dues, as aforesaid, or failing to comply with the above rules in any particular, will not be recognized or protected by the Colony.

This handbill invites black citizens in Lexington, Kentucky, to emigrate to Kansas. Those who made the journey often found better jobs and fairer laws than they had in the South.

1868 South Carolina constitutional convention. The poll tax also made it impossible for many poor whites to vote.

Even if he could pay the poll tax, each potential voter also had to prove he was literate by reading out loud a section of the state constitution. If he could not read, a (white) registrar would read the material to him, after which the voter had to explain what the passage meant. If the registrar decided that the man had not properly understood the passage, he could deny him the vote. This "understanding" clause gave voting officials a way to allow poor whites, many of whom were also illiterate or poorly educated, to vote, while barring black men.

Five states also passed laws requiring that a man own at least three hundred dollars' worth of property before he could vote. Since many black men did not own property, could not pay the poll tax, and could not read or write (at least not to white registrars' satisfaction), these restrictions barred huge numbers of voters from the ballot box.

Because thousands of poor, uneducated white men also could not meet the literacy or property qualifications, several southern states created loopholes that allowed them to vote. One such loophole was the "grandfather clause," which permitted an illiterate man, or one without property, to vote if he or an ancestor had voted *before* 1867. White men generally could meet this requirement, but since 1867 was the first year black men were permitted to vote, freedmen could not.

Poll taxes, literacy tests, understanding clauses, and property requirements worked all too well—by the turn of the century few black citizens in the South were still able to vote. Some state legislators defended the new laws by saying they excluded "unqualified" white as well as black citizens. Other legislators made no secret of their reason for supporting the voting restrictions. "There is no use to equivocate or lie about the matter," said James K. Vardaman, a Mississippi state senator. "Mississippi's constitutional convention [in 1890] was held for no other purpose than to eliminate the nigger from politics. . . . Let the world know it just as it is."

Many freedmen resisted efforts to rob them of their right to vote. Former slave and naval hero Robert Smalls, who had helped to write the 1868 South Carolina Constitution, was one of only six black delegates elected to his state's next constitutional convention in 1895. Smalls vigorously objected to proposals for a poll tax and literacy test, knowing what their effect would be, and to claims that freedmen were not fit to vote. "My race needs no special defense," he said, "for the past history of them in this country proves them to be the equal of any people anywhere. All they need is an equal chance in the battle of life."

When measures designed to keep blacks from voting were passed over his protests, Smalls traveled the country on a campaign to alert Americans to the "unnecessary and cruel laws" in South Carolina. Freedmen and women throughout the South joined Smalls in protesting the new laws; they wrote newspaper editorials, gave speeches, and appealed to officials in Washington, D.C., to protect black suffrage, all with no success.

Individually, many Northerners were angered by southern governments' efforts to keep black citizens from voting. But after the end of Reconstruction the federal government had declared a hands-off policy regarding southern politics. To justify federal inaction, government officials pointed out that the South's new laws did not *expressly* prohibit black men from voting.

But denying black citizens the vote, as well as dictating how and where they could work, was not enough for many southern whites. They wanted to make it impossible for former slaves to live as equals to whites. The "separate but equal" policies used by southern passenger railroads provided a way to accomplish this goal.

Southerners of both races relied on trains for basic transportation. Most trains had only two passenger cars, one for first-class ticket holders and a second car, often dirty and uncomfortable, for everyone else. Travelers, black and white, who could afford the cost preferred to ride in the comfort, cleanliness, and style of the first-class car.

But many white passengers who bought first-class tickets were offended at having to sit in the same car as black citizens. They began to complain to railway officials, and in some cases started brawls with black passengers.

To avoid trouble, some railroads started refusing to sell black passengers first-class tickets. Railroad officials in Alabama provided two first-class cars, one for white passengers, another for black travelers. But most railroads simply refused to seat black passengers in the better car, even if they held first-class tickets. Anyone who refused to move to the second-class car was put off the train at the next stop.

Many black travelers were outraged by such treatment. A number sued the railroads and railroad employees for discriminating against them, and sometimes won. But these legal victories had an unwelcome side effect. The courts began to decide that railroads could seat first-class black and white passengers in separate cars, as long as both cars provided the same level of comfort and quality.

Encouraged by these court decisions, one southern state after another passed separate but equal laws governing railroad travel. Since most railroads could not afford to outfit two first-class cars, in practice separate but equal meant that black passengers holding first-class tickets were seated in a section of the second-class car separated from the rest of the coach by a piece of cloth strung across the car. To black travelers forced to ride on them, the separate but equal cars quickly became known as "universally filthy and uncomfortable" symbols of "indignity, disgrace and shame."

When Louisiana passed a separate but equal law in 1890, two black men, lawyer and doctor Louis A. Martinet and activist Eli Freeman, decided to challenge not just the state law but the idea of segregation itself. Enlisting the help of a prominent northern white lawyer, Albion W. Tourgee, the men developed a plan. A black man named Homer Adolph Plessy would board the East Louisiana Railroad bound for Covington, Louisiana, and take a seat in the white coach. Railroad officials would be informed ahead of time that a black man would be boarding the whites-only car.

When questioned by the conductor, Plessy was to tell him that he was seven-eighths white. (In the eyes of the law, that meant he was black.) The conductor would tell Plessy to move to the second-class car, but he was to refuse and allow himself to be arrested. Tourgee then would bring a lawsuit on his behalf, charging the railroad and the state with interfering with Plessy's constitutional and human rights. They assumed they would lose the first round of the lawsuit, but hoped to win on appeal, where a favorable decision would have a much broader impact.

Events went exactly according to plan—for a while. When the

Under the separate but equal laws, blacks were forbidden to ride in the same railway cars, eat in the same restaurants, or shop at the same stores as white citizens. Here a train conductor orders a black man out of a first-class car.

case came to trial in 1892, the judge, as expected, decided that the state's separate but equal law was constitutional and ruled against Plessy. Tourgee immediately appealed the case to the state supreme court, where he also lost. Then, in December 1892, the U.S. Supreme Court agreed to hear the case. If the country's highest court ruled that the Louisiana segregation law was unconstitutional, the decision would provide a basis for overturning separate but equal laws throughout the South.

After a long delay, the Supreme Court heard the case on April 13, 1896. Tourgee and Plessy's two other attorneys argued that separate but equal laws were "an act of enforced discrimination catering to white supremacy and degrading the Negro." The laws also violated the equal protection clause of the Fourteenth Amendment, they said,

◆ Lynching ◆

The gruesome sight of a black man hanging by his neck from a bridge or tree was common in the South both during and after Reconstruction. Between 1889 and 1893, as many as seven hundred black men were "lynched" by white mobs without having been convicted of any crime.

Two black men from Georgia were lynched simply for "being Negroes." It was their misfortune to live near two other black men—who were also lynched—suspected of murdering a white family.

In some cases, black men charged with a crime but not yet tried in a court of law were lynched by white mobs. In 1884, three black men from Alabama were charged with setting fire to a barn and were put in jail. They were awaiting trial when, according to a story in the New York *Tribune*, "A mob of two hundred masked men entered the jail, after having enticed away the jailer with a false message, took the keys from the jailer's wife and secured the three prisoners. They were carried to a near-by bridge. Here a rope was placed around the neck of each victim, the other end being tied to

George Meadows was lynched in 1889 in Birmingham, Alabama.

the timbers of the bridge, and they were compelled to jump."

Members of lynch mobs were rarely brought to justice. Sometimes white authorities held a brief

which guaranteed that no persons could be discriminated against because of their race.

The majority of the Supreme Court justices was not swayed by the lawyers' passion or legal arguments and declared Louisiana's separate but equal law to be constitutional.

---

investigation, but they usually concluded that the victim had been killed by "parties unknown" and took no further action.

When three young black businessmen were lynched in Memphis, Tennessee, in 1892, a young editor at a local newspaper could no longer keep silent. Ida B. Wells, who was only twenty-three years old, was half-owner of the newspaper *Free Speech*. She wrote an editorial charging that several white businessmen, rivals of the three victims, were behind the lynchings.

An angry mob of white citizens retaliated by burning Wells's office and print shop. Members of the mob threatened to kill her unless she left town. Wells left Tennessee, moving to New York and then Chicago, but she did not stop speaking out against lynching. She launched a full-scale crusade, giving lectures nationwide and publishing pamphlets.

Ida B. Wells continued her campaign against lynching throughout her long public career. Before her death in 1931, she also helped found the National Association for the Advancement of Colored People, an influential organization that continues to aid black Americans.

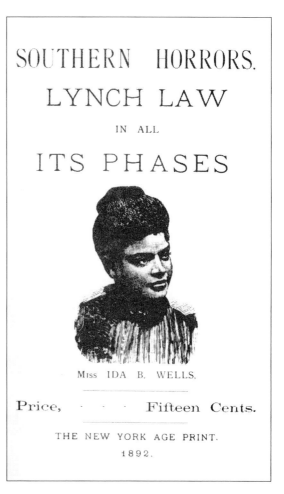

The cover of one of Ida B. Wells's anti-lynching pamphlets bears a portrait of its author. Wells gathered all her facts about lynchings from white-owned newspapers; she knew her statistics would not be believed if they came from black newspapers.

With its decision in *Plessy v. Ferguson*, the nation's highest court had put the official stamp of approval on the doctrine of separate but equal. Segregation was now legal. Meanwhile, in the four years between the time the Supreme Court agreed to hear the *Plessy* case and the time it issued its decision, all but three southern states had passed segregation laws. These laws applied not just to railroad travel but to almost every area of life where the two races might come in contact. The remaining three states—North Carolina, South Carolina, and Virginia—adopted segregation laws soon after the Supreme Court's ruling.

Before long, "for whites only" signs hung in the windows of restaurants, theaters, restrooms, and parks; black men and women were not even allowed to drink from the same water fountains as white men and women. And although separate, the "colored" facilities were almost never equal.

Black Americans continued to oppose and, where they could, fight segregation. But there was little they could do. Denied access to the ballot box, they could not protest through their votes. They could no longer expect help from the Republican party or the federal government. And black citizens who lobbied for change in the South discovered that speaking out for their rights could lead to being lynched—kidnapped by a white mob and hanged from the nearest tree, pole, or bridge railing. During the height of the lynching epidemic hundreds of black citizens were hanged to death by mobs.

Faced with such obstacles, most black Southerners simply tried to live as fully and with as much dignity as they could in their segregated society.

◆   ◆   ◆

Reconstruction was a period of great hope and crushing disappointment. Freedom did not bring former slaves the equality they had hoped for. And peace did not return the former Confederate states to their cherished way of life.

But important progress *was* made during Reconstruction, progress that helped lay the groundwork for momentous changes in American life. The Fourteenth and Fifteenth Amendments, which state that all Americans, regardless of race, are entitled to the same

Thirteenth Amendment (1865)

Section 1. Neither slavery nor involuntary servitude, except as a punishment for crime whereof the party shall have been duly convicted, shall exist within the United States, or any place subject to their jurisdiction.

Fourteenth Amendment (1868)

Section 1. All persons born or naturalized in the United States, and subject to the jurisdiction thereof, are citizens of the United States and of the state wherein they reside. No state shall make or enforce any law which shall abridge the privileges or immunities of citizens of the United States; nor shall any state deprive any person of life, liberty, or property, without due process of law; nor deny to any person within its jurisdiction the equal protection of the laws.

Fifteenth Amendment (1870)

Section 1. The right of citizens of the United States to vote shall not be denied or abridged by the United States or by any state on account of race, color, or previous condition of servitude.

The Thirteenth, Fourteenth, and Fifteenth Amendments to the U.S. Constitution are among the most enduring legacies of Reconstruction.

rights, were added to the Constitution. And Reconstruction gave rise to the black institutions—churches, schools, and community and political organizations—that supported the men and women who challenged and finally overturned segregation laws in the 1950s and 1960s.

In ways neither black nor white citizens of the time could appreciate, Reconstruction brought America closer to realizing the promise of equality for everyone.

❖ Glossary ❖

amendment   a change or addition to a constitution or law; an amendment to the U.S. Constitution must be ratified by three-fourths of the states before it becomes law

Black Codes   a series of laws, designed to limit the freedom of former slaves, passed by all-white legislatures in the southern states

bonds   redeemable certificates issued to the individuals, institutions, and governments that loaned money to the South or North to help finance the Civil War. Lenders expected to turn in the bonds at the end of the war and get their money back, with interest; most who had loaned funds to the Confederacy, however, were not repaid because the Confederacy lost the war and had no money.

carpetbaggers   the name conservative Southerners applied to Northerners who moved south during Reconstruction; the name was based on a stereotype of Northerners who arrived in the South with only one suitcase—a "carpetbag"—intending to stay in the region just long enough to profit from the South's misfortune and stir up trouble between whites and blacks

Confederate States of America   the alliance of eleven southern states that withdrew from the United States in 1860 and 1861; Alabama, Arkansas, Florida, Georgia, Louisiana, Mississippi, North Carolina, South Carolina, Tennessee, Texas, and Virginia

confiscated   seized; during the Civil War, the Union government confiscated land belonging to Confederates

conservative   during Reconstruction, another word for Democrat

Democrat   a member of the political party that had supported slavery and, during Reconstruction, generally fought efforts to expand the civil and voting rights of freedmen and women

emancipate to free from slavery

Fifteenth Amendment an amendment to the U.S. Constitution guaranteeing all men the right to vote, regardless of race; adopted in 1870

Fourteenth Amendment an amendment to the U.S. Constitution that forbids states to deprive citizens of life, liberty, or property without due process of law; adopted in 1868

freedman/freedwoman a freed slave

inaugurate to place an elected person into political office with a formal ceremony; for example, the president of the United States is elected in November and inaugurated in January

legislator a person who serves in a state or federal lawmaking body such as Congress

militia a group of citizens organized by a city or state for military service, especially during an emergency

plantation an estate or farm where crops are planted and harvested by large numbers of workers

polling place a place where people vote during an election

poll tax during and after Reconstruction, a tax people were required to pay before they could vote; the poll tax was often used to prevent poor people, especially former slaves, from voting

president-elect the term applied to newly elected presidents between the time they are elected and the time they actually take office; for example, the U.S. president is elected in November but does not take office until January

overseer a man hired by a plantation owner to supervise workers

Radical Reconstruction under this plan, supported by Radical Republicans in Congress, southern states were not allowed to rejoin the Union until they granted certain rights to former slaves; this plan was adopted over Presidential Reconstruction, which would have allowed southern states back into the Union without requiring them to extend additional rights to freedmen

ratify to formally approve, usually by a vote, a treaty, amendment, or other proposal

rebel another term for a Confederate soldier or a civilian supporter of the Confederacy

Reconstruction the period following the Civil War, during which the Union and the Confederacy became one country again

registrar   a person who records votes at a polling place

Republican   a member of the political party that opposed slavery and, during Reconstruction, supported policies to expand the voting and civil rights of freed slaves

scalawag   a scornful term applied by conservative Southerners to white Southerners who supported the Republican party during Reconstruction

suffrage   the right to vote

textiles   woven or knit cloth—such as cotton, wool, and linen—produced in factories and used to make clothing and other goods

Thirteenth Amendment   an amendment to the U.S. Constitution that outlaws slavery anywhere in the United States; adopted in December 1865

Union   another name for the United States of America, used especially during the Civil War

veteran   a former member of one of the armed services

vigilantes   individuals or groups who take the law into their own hands and punish a person accused of a crime before that person has a chance to defend himself in a court of law

war debt   the amount of money a country owes after having borrowed money to finance a war

Yankee   another name for a Northerner

❖ Further Reading ❖

Berlin, Ira, et al., eds. *Free at Last: A Documentary History of Slavery, Freedom, and the Civil War*. New York: The New Press, 1992.

Bowen, Clarissa Adger. *The Diary of Clarissa Adger Bowen: Ashtabula Plantation, 1865*. Edited by Allan Nevia and Milton Halsey Thomas. New York: The Macmillan Company, 1952.

Cumming, Kate. *Kate: The Journal of a Confederate Nurse*. Edited by Richard Barksdale Harwell. Baton Rouge, La.: Louisiana State University Press, 1959.

Foner, Eric. *Reconstruction: America's Unfinished Revolution, 1863–1877*. New York: Harper & Row, 1988.

LeConte, Emma. *When the World Ended: The Diary of Emma LeConte*. Edited by Earl Schenck Miers. Lincoln, Nebr.: University of Nebraska Press, 1987.

Litwack, Leon. *Been in the Storm So Long: The Aftermath of Slavery*. New York: Vintage Books, 1980.

Magdol, Edward. *A Right to the Land: Essays on the Freedmen's Community*. Westport, Conn.: Greenwood Press, 1977.

McPherson, James M. *Ordeal by Fire, Volume III: Reconstruction*. New York: Alfred A. Knopf, 1982.

Reid, Whitelaw. *After the War: A Southern Tour, May 1, 1865, to May 1, 1866*. New York: Moore, Wilstach & Baldwin, 1866.

Roark, James L. *Masters Without Slaves: Southern Planters in the Civil War and Reconstruction*. New York: W. W. Norton & Company, 1977.

Sterling, Dorothy. *Captain of the Planter: The Story of Robert Smalls, 1839–1915*. New York: Oxford University Press, 1971.

———. *The Trouble They Seen: Black People Tell the Story of Reconstruction*. Garden City, N.Y.: Doubleday & Company, 1976.

Strong, George Templeton. *The Diary of George Templeton Strong: Post-War Years, 1865–1875*. Edited by Allan Nevia and Milton Halsey Thomas. New York: The Macmillan Company, 1952.

Swint, Henry Lee. *The Northern Teacher in the South, 1862–1870*. New York: Octagon Books, 1967.

Trowbridge, J. T. *The South: A Tour of its Battle-fields and Ruined Cities, A Journey Through the Desolated States, and Talks with the People*. Hartford, Conn.: L. Stebbins, 1866.

Vaughn, William Preston. *Schools for All: The Blacks & Public Education in the South, 1865–1877*. Lexington, Ky.: The University Press of Kentucky, 1974.

Waterbury, Maria. *Seven Years Among the Freedmen*. Chicago: T. B. Arnold, 1891. Reprint. Freeport, N.Y.: Books for Libraries Press, 1971.

Wells-Barnett, Ida B. *On Lynchings: Southern Horrors; A Red Record; Mob Rule in New Orleans*. New York: Arno Press and The New York Times, 1969.

Woodward, C. Vann. *Reunion and Reaction: The Compromise of 1877 and the End of Reconstruction*. New York: Oxford University Press, 1966.

✦ Acknowledgments ✦

Boundless thanks to Steven Miller of the Freedmen and Southern Society Project at the University of Maryland. He steered me toward the best sources, answered every question, read every version of the manuscript, and offered consistently useful criticism and advice. And he was always patient and good-humored.

I also want to salute the patience and persistence of the staff at the prints and photographs division of the Library of Congress, who spent countless hours helping me locate obscure photographs and illustrations. Thanks are also due to John and Troy Leib of Leib Image Archives, Eleanor Richardson at the South Caroliniana Library, Pat Hash at the South Carolina Historical Society, Suellyn Lathrop at the Kansas State Historical Society, and Michael P. Musick at the National Archives.

I'm grateful to the folks who read the manuscript in draft and provided me with invaluable comments: Peggy Denker, Jenice View, Deborah Bouton, Michelle Lamboy, Cheryl Russell, and Pamela Wilson. Special thanks to Edna Medford of Howard University and her daughter Lark, and to Valerie Wilk, who was always willing to listen.

❖ Index ❖

Page numbers in *italics* refer to photographs and illustrations.

118

✦ Picture Credits ✦

The photographs and illustrations in this book are from the following sources. The images are public domain or are used with the source's permission.

Boston Public Library • pages 50, 65

Chicago Historical Society • page 8

Freedmen and Southern Society Project, College Park, Md. • pages 18, 35, 48, 52, 84

Harper's Weekly (Oct. 21, 1876) • page 89

Kansas State Historical Society, Topeka, Kans. • page 103

Leib Image Archives, York, Pa. • pages ii, viii, 9, 21, 45, 73, 74, 77, 82, 95

Library of Congress, Washington, D.C. • pages 3, 7, 11, 15, 25, 29, 31, 32, 33, 38, 41, 44, 49, 55, 58, 63, 66 (both), 68, 76, 78, 85, 86, 92, 94, 96–97, 98, 101, 107, 108

National Museum of American History, Smithsonian Institution, Washington, D.C. • page 16

On Lynchings: Southern Horrors; A Red Record; Mob Rule in New Orleans (Ayer Company Publications, North Stratford, N.H.) • page 109

South Caroliniana Library, University of South Carolina, Columbia, S.C. • pages 4–5

U.S. Army Military History Institute, Carlisle Barracks, Pa. • pages 42, 57